Letting Magic In

ALSO BY MAIA TOLL

The Night School

The Wild Wisdom Companion

The Illustrated Crystallery

The Illustrated Bestiary

The Illustrated Herbiary

Letting Magic In

a memoir of becoming

MAIA TOLL

RUNNING PRESS

PHILADELPHIA

Running Press
Hachette Book Group
1290 Avenue of the Americas, New York, NY 10104
www.runningpress.com
@Running_Press

Printed in the United States of America

First Edition: June 2023

Published by Running Press, an imprint of Perseus Books, LLC, a subsidiary of Hachette Book Group, Inc. The Running Press name and logo are trademarks of the Hachette Book Group.

The Hachette Speakers Bureau provides a wide range of authors for speaking events. To find out more, go to www.hachettespeakersbureau.com or email HachetteSpeakers@hbgusa.com.

Running Press books may be purchased in bulk for business, educational, or promotional use. For more information, please contact your local bookseller or the Hachette Book Group Special Markets Department at Special.Markets@hbgusa.com.

The publisher is not responsible for websites (or their content) that are not owned by the publisher.

Print book cover and interior design by Susan Van Horn

LCCN: 2022043614

ISBNs: 978-0-7624-8041-8 (hardcover), 978-0-7624-8043-2 (ebook)

LSC-C

Printing 1, 2023

To those who first found magic in the pages of a book.

Contents

Introduction

Practicing magic takes a kind of awareness you don't feel ordinarily ... You have to really know things around you and make them know you. And when you manage that connection, it's as though the world belongs to you. You feel more at home in it.

—Emily Croy Barker, *The Thinking Woman's Guide to Real Magic*

In ancient times magic was not thought to be supernatural or paranormal, it was seen as the capacity to bring creative thought into physical reality.

—Jessica Dawn Palmer, *Animal Wisdom*

IN 2016, I GAVE MYSELF A WEEKLONG WRITING RETREAT IN
Carmel, California.

Each day I'd set up my makeshift desk on a picnic table in the garden. The
air was rich with rosemary, sharp with sea salt. Other scents ghosted through
my mind—black tea and rose geranium oil, the honey-sweet smell of hot wax,
the musk of manure. As I typed, memories of a year I'd spent in Ireland gently draped themselves over the California landscape.

I have no photos from that time. My teacher—an herbalist and self-
described witch—had told us to put our cameras away and be present in the
moment. So, instead, my nose took snapshots: the grassy smell of drying nettles, the unexpected citrus snap of clary sage crushed carelessly underfoot.
As I was clicking at my keyboard in Carmel, the scents of Ireland became
scenes. Scenes became chapters. A through-line began to appear and, along
with it, a hopeful thought: *maybe, just maybe, I've begun drafting a book.*

In the evenings, the seven women on retreat would come together, gathering by the fire to read aloud from our day's work. Afterward, my roommate
and I would sleepily climb the stairs to our room on the second floor. Sliding open the glass door, I'd step out onto the balcony. Below, the driveway
twisted down through sea pines and cedar. The moon's trail rippled as the
Pacific stretched and sighed in the distance. Each night my roommate and
I would take full advantage of this enchantment, using it to set an intention
for our dreams.

One night, midweek, I sat on my single bed, grounding into my feet and
stretching through my crown. On the nightstand, I'd already placed an open
notebook and pen as invitations to my subconscious. Breathing in and out, I
settled. My mind wandered to the writing I'd been doing. It was beginning to
feel like the start of a memoir. *What should the title be?* I mused. Giving in to
whimsy, I used that thought to set my intention.

I awoke to seabirds carousing beyond the balcony. Vaguely, I remembered scrawling something in the dark hours before dawn. Was that a
memory? A dream? I felt around for my spiral-bound notebook, which had

fallen to the floor. As I leaned over the edge of the bed to retrieve it, I saw words dashed off in blue ink:

Letting Magic In.

Letting Magic In. . . .

In the years since the Carmel retreat, I've rolled these words on my tongue, testing the taste of them. I've asked: *What exactly is magic?* What do *I* mean by *magic*? This is not a new question for me, but instead one I've been pondering in one form or another since I was young. My answer usually revolves around feelings for which I can't find language: What is the word for craving a relationship with the earth, plants, rocks, and stars? What do you call someone who finds their spirit sparked by these connections, whose concept of the sacred is altered by the scent of jasmine in bloom or the deep indigo of a sky awaiting nightfall? We're taught that doctors know our bodies and clergy know our souls. But what if you're a person seeking to understand both for yourself without an intermediary? What is the word for these feelings and the person we become when we honor them?

We don't have good language to help us name and address the longing for a life that's richer and truer than the one we're currently leading. So, while the word *magic* is, perhaps, not quite right, I've realized it points to a gnawing craving for a connection that includes, but also stretches beyond, the human realm. It's the word I use to mark those moments when I allow myself to lean into my intuition, to revel in synchronicity, to be in awe of mystery, and to sink into the cycles that exist outside of myself.

Sometimes magic has felt like a cosmic zap, and I've known immediately that something notable has shifted within me. But often magic has snuck in without me being consciously aware of it, nesting like a mouse in a forgotten corner of my mind, chewing through outdated neural wiring and making a mess of what I previously thought of as oh-so-logical. The trick, it seems, is learning how to come to center, to find one's balance through both the huge revelations and the tiny but persistent shifts.

As I was finding my personal equilibrium between these two poles, there were times when I felt like the Fool from the tarot deck, stepping blithely over the cliff's edge. The beginning of my journey was confusing; the middle was messy. Western culture doesn't have a model for the deep interiority required to attune to our inner senses. The process can be—and was!—unsettling. Luckily, I found mentors who both allowed me to find my way and gave me a stern talking-to when I wallowed in the muck. Sometimes I got yanked back into prevailing cultural precepts. Other times I felt silly or judged by other people. I questioned myself, wondering if I was a little crazy or a lot weird. Then I learned that in Middle English, *weird* referred to one who could control fate. And isn't that what we all want? To be weird enough to take control of our own lives? To know who we are and what we are becoming? To be willing to choose an outlook that allows life to be a joyous adventure?

As my thinking shifted, I began to see patterns. I started to feel how my inner world reflected the outer world and vice versa. I noticed the cycles swirling around me—the seasons, the moons, my own breath—and began to work with them to create flow and balance. I realized that I was crafting something very important with my every thought: *my own life.*

When I look back, even seemingly insignificant moments can be strung together, allowing me—and you!—to see the beadwork of the larger story, a journey that began in my childhood but gained momentum in my thirtieth year when I moved from Brooklyn to the small town of Beacon, New York. During my three years in Beacon—which spanned the unexpected and tragic events that centered on September 11, 2001—I learned to use my sixth sense, or intuition, as a doorway to the inner realms. Through this work, I developed a profound ability to trust myself, which allowed me to make large and wondrous changes in my life. These changes culminated in selling my house in Beacon and moving across the ocean. To study with a witch. In Ireland.

While my hours typing away in the garden during the writing retreat in Carmel helped me begin this book, my focus then had been on Ireland. It's easy, even for me, to romanticize "witch school" on the Emerald Isle. But as I dug deeper, it became clear that the most essential parts of the story happened *before* I traveled across the sea. I realized that Ireland was possible only because I'd gone through a series of transformations in the years leading up to that trip.

What were the steps to becoming a person who believed in herself enough, who trusted her intuition enough, who could feel the pull of life's currents enough, that she could find the courage to allow herself to step off the mapped edge? To believe that she could live that kind of magic?

This book is about that becoming. It's about how I learned to let magic in so I could live the life I longed for—one filled with curiosity, connection, and the deepest kind of inner knowing. It's about the things that change you in unexpected ways and guide you to become the person you never knew you wanted to be but, perhaps, always were.

A Note

The memories recorded here are as accurate as I can make them, but if you've ever held a memory, you know they tend to change a little with each touch. These particular memories have been handled many times over the intervening decades: they are the roots of who I've become. Reading through my old journals, I'm surprised how memory has sculpted and resculpted past events without my being consciously aware of the shifts. I've navigated these discrepancies as best I can, while keeping in mind that sometimes the story as it evolved is more important to understanding the journey than the specifics of the original moment.

Pseudonyms have been liberally sprinkled throughout. A memoir is one person's perception of a particular moment in history. We should all be allowed to change and grow, not be suspended forever in the amber of someone else's tale.

Another Note

Early in the writing, a friend noted the weblike quality of the scenes I'd chosen to share, how they seem disparate until late in the book when the entirety of the pattern was revealed. With that one conversation, spiderweb imagery wove its way into my consciousness. I began researching arachnids and how they do what they do.

Spiders weave with seven different silks. There are silks for spiraling and silks for sticking, silks for structure and silks for securing. These streamers are produced from seven different glands within the spider's body.

The weaving begins with a thin line secreted from the ampullate gland. One end is secured where the spider is standing, the other cast outward on the wind. The spider rides the breeze, attaching the silk wherever it lands. Then it crosses back over this tightrope, dropping a line from the center point. It rappels down this new streamer, attaching it to the ground. The web now has three anchors.

Point by point, silk by silk, the spider weaves its web. It looks like nothing at first: a three-legged stool, a child's sketch of a snowflake. But keep watching! Slowly the spiral forms and a pattern becomes apparent.

This is the way my mind works, so it seemed fitting that this book evolved in much the same way. And when I reflected on it, I realized this is also how many people experience a mystical awakening: moments of magic are strung together in a seemingly random array until the seeker can step back far enough to see the greater pattern. The anchor points might seem odd at first, with the outer spiral broad and looping as time whirls like a kaleidoscope, stopping *here*, and *here*, and *here*. But, if you are patient, point by point, connection by connection, the journey emerges.

Prologue
1980–1991

I'VE DONE EVERYTHING IN MY POWER TO FORGET THE experience of overnight camp: the mean girls who taunted me for being chubby, the nurse who made me run on an injured ankle, the niggling suspicion I'd been sent away, not for my own benefit, but so my parents could have a vacation. In all fairness, they needed it: Dad was working eighty hours a week growing his law firm, and Mom . . . Mom was trying to find herself. That, I have learned, is a difficult and consuming process. Still, my ideal summer would have been spent at the small day camp run by the farm where I took riding lessons. I wasn't any better at horseback riding than tennis or softball, mind you, but I had a primal, and somewhat inexplicable, yearning to be near horses—a need no one in my family understood, including me. But I was compelled by some inner knowing and fought, both wildly and staunchly, to be allowed to respond. I won the battle for riding lessons during the school year, but when summer came, I lost the fight.

The camp was in the Pocono Mountains of Pennsylvania. Although I can't tell you who was in my cabin or which sports made me most miserable, I can confirm that camp did give me one immeasurable gift.

It was my third summer. I was in Bunk J on a hill accessed by a flight of nearly one hundred steps that we had to troop up and down to get to the lake, the archery field, and the dining hall. Girls in white shorts and shirts flew past me, hair in braids and ponytails, voices bouncing and laughing. They were a flight of gazelles, streaming up, up, up. Then down, down, down.

7

After we had swum in the silt-bottomed lake and eaten three raucous meals at the long tables of the dining hall, we were finally allowed to shower and curl up in our squeaky metal beds. As the lights flickered out along the row of cabins, a velvety blackness would descend upon the hilltop, broken only by the calling of the counselors' voices and the beams of their flashlights bobbing down the hundred steps. Beyond the window screens, fireflies flickered, while inside the cabin girls giggled and murmured. Then my counselor's penlight would click on, her voice warming the darkness:

TARAN WANTED *to make a sword; but Coll, charged with the practical side of his education, decided on horseshoes. And so it had been horseshoes all morning long . . .*

The Book of Three by Lloyd Alexander. Every night our counselor gave us the gift of just a few pages before whispering "good night" and slipping out to do counselor things. Some of the other girls speculated on what these things might be and which male counselor might be involved. I didn't. I lay there on my thin, squeaky bed and thought about Taran and Hen Wen the oracular pig. I considered whatever magic had been revealed in the evening's reading. Was it real? Were there people out in the world right now imbuing objects with power and slipping into truth-revealing trances?

I became determined to find out.

Late in July, when my parents picked me and my sister up from camp, we still had not reached the conclusion of *The Book of Three*. I'm sure most of my bunk went home and forgot about Taran. Their tween years were filled with Nancy Drew and Sweet Valley High. But Lloyd Alexander's words had wriggled into my subconscious, unlocking doors and opening windows. The world felt bigger, somehow, more filled with possibility.

Back in the car on the way home from camp, I was at the very beginning of what would become a life's quest. But I didn't know that then. The only thing that was clear to me was that I had to find out how *The Book of Three*

8

ended. I demanded we stop at Barnes & Noble. My mother twisted in the passenger seat to stare at me.

"*You* want to go to the bookstore?" she asked, eyebrows raised. At that point I didn't really read. While I'd learned the mechanics of it—I was eleven after all!—reading was yet another thing for which I had little natural aptitude.

"I need to know what happens to Taran and Hen Wen," I confirmed.

"Then we'll go tomorrow!" Mom promised, beaming at my father.

After that I was rarely without a book. They were all of a type: J.R.R. Tolkien, C. S. Lewis, Ursula Le Guin, Madeleine L'Engle. I learned about magic while slurping spaghetti, a book balanced beyond my plate. When I was dragged to synagogue, I tucked a novel inside my prayer book. Once I had my driver's license, I'd read at stoplights, a book propped against the steering wheel.

As I read, I became increasingly convinced that the authors of the world were tapped into something special. At first it was enough to experience enchantment on the page, in the world of a book. But as I got older, I began to wonder if magic could be found, not just in stories, but also in everyday life. Signs were scarce; there was no magic or mysticism in my formal education and my searches through the library's back-stacks were fruitless.

Senior year in high school, I packed a new acquisition into my backpack—Douglas Adams's *The Hitchhiker's Guide to the Galaxy*. My determination hadn't waned: magic was out there, and even if I had to explore the far reaches of the universe, I was going to find it! Imagine my surprise when, two decades later, I learned that the thing I had been seeking wasn't hidden in a restaurant at the end of the universe but was, instead, residing somewhere much, much closer to home....

Brooklyn, NY

1998–1999

1

There are many herbs to repel spirits: sage, rue, oregano, and thyme
will all do the trick. Saint-John's-wort will bring light to dark spaces
and holly will snag ghosts on its tiny thorns.

Jan had been dead for two weeks.

The man who lived in the brownstone next door kept mistaking me for her, yelling "Hi, Jan!" from his upstairs window as I left for school in the morning. With my cropped hair, I suppose it was an easy mistake, especially if you didn't know either of us well. We both had dark curls: mine were short for ease, hers for chemo. Still, each time I was called by her name, my stomach would chill, and the thought would flutter through my mind: *Jan is dead and I am her ghost.*

The year before, we'd known each other just enough to say "hi" in the hallways of the Illustrious Private School where we both taught. We'd occasionally chat about nothings: the colored pencil selection in the art closet or how the salad bar had run out of olives before we'd had our lunch break.

While I hadn't known Jan well enough to hear her grumbling about the cost of a new roof or the ridiculous price of gutters, Claire certainly had. Claire was Jan's best friend and the head of the Lower School where I taught. A small woman with fawn-colored hair and a gentle smile, Claire valued quirky thoughts and had very definite ideas about what might be good for someone else. At other points in my life, this definitiveness would have annoyed me. But I was betwixt and between—after being diagnosed with a learning disability, I'd dropped out of architecture school and moved to New York City with few friends beyond my (now ex) girlfriend. To make things more topsy-turvy, I was on eggshells with my family after the debacle of coming out as bisexual.

All this to say, there wasn't much ground that felt solid.

Claire, the mother of a grad school friend, had offered me a job at the Illustrious Private School. It felt like I was stepping into a ready-made community, and I was immensely grateful. Like an exhausted rescue pup, I leaned into Claire for support and guidance. So when my girlfriend and I broke up—leaving me without a place to live—it was easy to let Claire handle it. And she did . . . by convincing Jan to let me rent the disused apartment in her brownstone's basement.

Despite being desperate—finding an apartment in Brooklyn on short notice is rarely easy—I blinked back tears as I eyed the thick dust on the baseboards and the baroque burgundy wallpaper. *Why did **she** get to keep the apartment?* I thought, suddenly angry. I'd found the sunlit second-floor walk-up my girlfriend and I had shared. Now I was contemplating life in a gloomy basement because, even after she cheated on me, I couldn't bear the thought of *her* ending up in a gloomy basement apartment.

Shaking my head at my own ridiculousness, I walked through the dimly lit front room, entering a surprisingly generous kitchen. There were fifties plywood cabinets against one wall and a door that led outside; I peered through its window into a well-loved garden. The Japanese maple in the center rustled in an unseen breeze. My shoulders unhitched a little. Maybe this would be okay. Experimentally, I walked to the sink and turned on the tap. The water sputtered, running brown.

Braced against the sink, my back to Claire, I closed my eyes and considered my options. Clearly the apartment hadn't been lived in for decades. And Jan seemed prickly about having a renter; it was obvious she'd been talked into it. But the truth was I didn't have any other prospects. Plus, Claire was delighted: her best friend (Jan) and her protégé (me) would both be right across the street from her!

I turned from the sink as Claire gestured toward the flocked wallpaper. "We'll paint this antique white," she said crisply. "It looks wretched now, but it will be rather nice. You'll see." She smiled.

So I gave Jan a deposit.

The first week of summer break, Claire and I primed and painted. Jan looked on stoically, hands on her hips, her black tank top spotless.

But as the summer progressed, Jan began to thaw. We gardened together or grabbed takeout from the Chinese place on the corner. The school year began. We sometimes had a drink after work, sitting on her cozy antique sofa surrounded by the begonias she'd grown to gargantuan size.

Jan was diagnosed with cancer in November. It was unexpected and fast moving. I made myself useful when I could—which was rarely. Even ill, Jan insisted she needed no one. We saw each other less and less.

One unusually warm day in late February, a few months into her chemo treatments, she came out to the garden where I was drinking my morning coffee. She pointed to this and that, going over care instructions casually, as if she were Martha Stewart telling an interviewer the growth habits of her favorite peonies. She was softer, folding in on herself. It was like watching a star collapse.

———————

I assumed Claire would be the one to tell me when Jan died. But that's not what happened. Instead, the Lower School's administrative assistant, a woman named Anna, casually mentioned Jan's passing while I was in the office making tea. It was March 31. Jan had died in the night. The electric kettle steamed, and I mechanically poured water over my tea bag before thanking Anna for the news just like I did when she handed me a stack of messages, each neatly written on a slip from the pink notepad. *While you were out . . .*

While you were out, Jan passed away.

Except I wasn't out. I was downstairs in my apartment fast asleep. For months I'd been wondering what death would sound like, what my role would be when Jan passed.

Apparently, your role was to sleep, I said to myself sarcastically.

I upended the honey bear and squeezed. The honey overflowed the spoon's bowl, dripping into the tea. I kept adding more, mesmerized by the amber liquid. My head was weirdly light, and something was bubbling up from my chest, trying to escape. It *almost* felt like relief. Which was *not* okay. I turned my back to Anna as I panted through the moment, trying to slow my inhale, to send air to all the spaces that had been tight and anaerobic for months. Jan's impending death had been a constant worry. Would we be home alone when it happened? Would I hear her fall and run upstairs to find her collapsed on the floor, watched over by the massive begonias?

Now, she was gone . . . and I'd slept right through it.

The feeling high in my chest became a tickle. I wanted to scrub at it, but the sticky spoon was in one hand, the honey bear in the other. Behind me the phone rang, and Anna answered sweetly, "Lower School. How may I help you?"

It seemed absurd that I had woken up in Jan's house and gotten dressed for work without knowing she was gone. The night my ex-girlfriend's cat died, I had a dream. In the morning, I knew the cat had passed.

I had expected to *know*—somehow, on a metaphysic level—when Jan died.

Mechanically, I squeezed the bear's belly one more time, adding another splat of honey. Taking a slow, controlled breath, I threw away the sticky spoon and screwed the lid onto my travel mug to keep the tea safe as I traversed the many stairs between the office and my classroom. I still had to teach. It wasn't like the school was going to close for the day.

My tea was undrinkably sweet, but it would take me many hours to notice.

———————

Throughout the day—as Hallie, my assistant teacher, arrived toting a heavy sling bag and a venti coffee from Starbucks, as the kids gathered on the purple rug to learn how to add fractions, as I locked myself in the bathroom to put Visine in my eyes one more time—I listened for Claire.

15

I hadn't seen much of her in the past month. She'd seemed withdrawn when we did meet, and I'd felt a nagging fear even as I told myself that her distance was due to concern for Jan. But now that it was over, now that Jan was gone, surely Claire would stop by. We'd make a plan to meet later at her place. Her husband would pour us red wine, then slump in his chair, legs sprawled, while Claire and I curled up on either end of the sofa. He would nod sagely as I confessed the relief I initially felt when I heard Jan had passed. And Claire? Claire would understand. Then she would tell stories about Jan, and we'd laugh and cry and find something akin to comfort.

But the footsteps never paused as people cruised by my classroom. No one peered around the door, elf like, to offer a sad smile.

After the last bell, Hallie and I put the chairs up on the desks so the room could be mopped.

"Did Claire tell you?" Hallie asked, hefting a chair with one hand. I knew she was talking about Jan.

"No," I scooped my hand to catch the shreds I was brushing from the table. One of the boys confetti-ed paper when he got anxious. "I found out in the office, when I went for tea."

Hallie froze, a small blue chair hoisted halfway.

"Oh shit. I'm sorry, Em," Like most people at school, she used my nickname. I had started spelling it out—*Em*, not *M*.

I rested my forehead on the seat of an orange plastic chair, the perfect height now that it was perched on the table.

"I guess it's official," I said to the laminated tabletop. "She's not talking to me. I just wish I knew why." I scrubbed at my eyes. They felt puffy under my fingertips.

Hallie's hair curtained her face as she turned away and briskly lifted the remaining chairs onto the last round table. There was something in the set of her shoulders—rounded, like a bird mantling. "Hal? What do you know? Is she still angry about the dog-sitting thing? I told her I had to go home that weekend…"

16

Hallie was shaking her head, a tiny side to side that set her hair to swinging. "I don't know. But I heard—and I don't know if this is true—that it's because of you and Jan . . ."

"Me and Jan?" I repeated, confused.

Hallie just looked at me, one eyebrow raised while she waited.

It took me a moment to absorb the innuendo. *Me and Jan?* "Wait . . . No! It wasn't like that!"

But Jan had been Claire's closest friend. And now she was gone. I tried to imagine what Claire might be feeling, what she might be thinking. But all I could feel was loss, tugging at me like an undertow. I wasn't even sure *which* loss was pulling me down: the loss of Jan or the loss of Claire. It was strange to discover that my heart actually hurt a bit, that heartache wasn't simply a metaphor. I'd experienced this sensation before and forgotten. I was taken off guard all over again by the physicality of the pain.

I don't recall the walk home from school. It was early spring, so the gingkoes were probably splashed in lime green. Most likely I tripped at the spot, a block from the house, where the sidewalk had buckled over the roots of a long-gone street tree. (I tripped there almost daily, so it's easy to imagine.) When I got home, I'm sure the gate squealed as I pulled it back and perhaps my key jammed as I jiggled it in the lock. And then I was in the hallway. The hallway lit by one bare bulb, which flickered a little as I entered.

"Jan?" I whispered.

But the house was silent.

———

By morning, the silence had taken on weight, spilling from the upper floors, dripping down the walls of my little basement apartment. I needed air. *Starbucks for breakfast,* I decided, swinging into my coat and shouldering my bag. My skin tingled, a light frisson up my spine. *I'm in a house where someone diiieeed,* one part of my brain moaned. *Stop creeping yourself out! And, besides, you have no idea where Jan died; it most likely happened at the hospi-tal,* the prim part of my mind admonished and redirected my focus to coffee. Maybe I'd treat myself to a latte.

On the way out of the house, I flipped on the hall light. After teaching, I had an appointment with my thesis adviser at NYU—I had decided to give graduate school another go—and I wasn't sure I'd make it home before dark. The portico was always shadowed, but after sunset it was near impossible to see the keyhole without the light from that friendly little bulb shining through the grated window.

Jan had been adamant about not wasting electricity, so leaving the light on—which I did regularly—had become a thing. I could picture her leaning over the railing, her lanky body forming a right triangle with the banister as she checked for the telltale glow. She must have performed these gymnastics often because the light was rarely on when I returned home. The bulb had become an ongoing argument, albeit one without words. My stomach gave a little twist as I flicked the switch. "Sorry, Jan," I murmured to the empty air. Swallowing unexpected tears, I adjusted the strap of my shoulder bag and headed down the hallway.

As I got to the door, I looked back before stepping out of the silence and into the bursting blue of a Brooklyn morning.

That evening, I crammed in with the commuters to return to Brooklyn. The packed subway car smelled of gyros and french fries. My stomach grumbled and I surreptitiously looked around to see if anyone had noticed. The meeting with my adviser had gone as well as expected. I was tepid about the whole thesis thing and having trouble choosing a topic. I had been twenty-four years old when I dropped out of architecture school after being diagnosed with a learning disability and advised "to reevaluate my professional goals." NYU had transferred my credits. Once I completed the current semester, I'd be just a thesis away from a master's degree.

Gripping the railing, I stomped up the steps from the subway platform, aiming for the rectangle of evening sky I could see over the heads of the Wall Street commuters. I was a bit of a school junkie, probably because I still hoped that there was some mystical instruction manual buried deep in the university library's back stacks. Yes, more than a decade since Taran and the *Hitchhiker's Guide to the Galaxy* I was still searching for *something*. I'd peruse the oldest shelves on a regular basis, running an index finger over the spines, sometimes opening a book to read a sentence at random.

But it was more than a search for magic that kept me matriculated: As long as I stayed in school, I didn't have to choose my next steps or declare a life path; I could remain in the in-between. Plus, being a student was something I knew how to do.

Soon there was only me and a pair of musicians left on the sidewalk. They were a few strides ahead, one carrying a guitar case, the other something smaller. I shoved my hands into my coat pockets. It was an old coat, and I felt the vintage lining give way.

"Shit," I muttered. The woman swung her head around and a dark-kohled eye peeked out from under her magenta hair. She looked me up and down, decided my problem was nothing she could help with, nodded, and kept going.

I fingered the inside of the pocket. I'd already resewn it twice, the pink thread standing out against the lining's sienna silk. I was beginning to wonder if there was enough fabric left to fix it again. I wasn't good at giving stuff up, as my mom often pointed out. She'd finger the holes in my sweatshirts and the rips in my jeans, her face a portrait of disapproval.

At my corner, the mafia lookout was on his stoop, smoking a cigarette. My Georgia boots sang *clump, clump, clump* as the sidewalk changed from cement to worn slate pavers. Daffodils glowed white behind wrought-iron railings. Down the street, Claire's house was lit up and cozy. Someone in a long, dark coat was waiting on her stoop balancing what looked like a Pyrex baking pan on the railing. The person knocked, pausing on the threshold until the door opened, and then that someone—that someone who wasn't

19

me—was welcomed inside. My heart gave a sad little thump, the achiness I'd once again forgotten about suddenly returning. I tucked myself into the shadow of a scrubby street tree, careful not to trample the tulips someone had planted around it.

As I stood watching, a few more people walked up the steps. In the evening gloom, I saw the distinctive stoop of Nathaniel, the school's headmaster, and then a woman I was fairly certain was Hallie, in her usual hoodie and yoga pants. Cars pulled up and their headlights flicked off. Shadowy forms fished bottles of wine and containers of food from back seats and wheel wells. I stayed against the tree, willing myself to be invisible. Tears streaked my cheeks; I ignored them till they began to drip down my neck, then felt around the rip in my pocket for a tissue. Would someone invite me in if they saw me?

But it was irrelevant; no one noticed me. I waited until the street emptied, then hurried down the steps to the lower-level door of Jan's house and fished out my key. After letting myself in, I carefully locked the gate. Fingers trailing lightly along the wall (painted the antique white Claire had chosen), I shrugged my book bag off my shoulder, pausing and closing my eyes for just a moment. Tears leaked from behind my lids.

I was about to open the door into my apartment when the hall light, the one I'd left on, flickered. Not the usual dying-light-bulb spit and pop but something more like a pulse. I froze, goose bumps crawling up my arms. My breath came short and quick as I yanked the door open, fumbling for the interior light switch. *What was that?* My heart was thumping, vibrating all the way down to my wrists.

I leaned against the closed door, trying to calm my breathing. *Do I believe in ghosts?* I asked myself. I thought about phoning my mom, but Mom was funny about this kind of thing—like she wanted to believe but didn't at the same time. Still, I felt more comfortable with the cordless phone in my hand.

———————

As April turned to May, the bulb continued to pulse. It was like Morse code in light form. *Long-long-long-short!* the bulb would announce.

In many ways, I had more of a relationship with the memory of Jan than I'd had with Jan herself. We'd only been an active part of each other's lives for a few months before she was diagnosed, and after that it all went quickly.

Adrift in Jan's brownstone, mistaken for a dead woman by the neighbors and shut out from the house across the street, my grief became tangled and twisted. I replayed moments from the past nine months over and over: I had sat with Jan the evening she'd shorn her hair. We drank wine and munched on olives in her living room. Had she wanted to share that intimate moment with me specifically, or was I just the person who happened to be around, the one who lived in her basement? When I pushed to be included on the speakers' list at the school's memorial service, I'd heard the murmurs: *she hasn't known Jan for long; she was just the renter.*

Maybe that was true; maybe I had no right to mourn Jan.

So, instead, I talked to the light bulb and grieved for myself. The Lower School orbited around Claire and she was hardly speaking to me. I was no longer lauded at faculty meetings or asked to help with new curriculum. And when a parent complained about something, I was no longer defended. I'd fallen off my protégé pedestal. The bulb offered a bit of solace and, oddly, a sense of connection. *Long-long!* it would comment in its Morse code–like flickering, as I flipped its switch before heading out the door. I would smile at the bulb and say, "I hear you, Jan." Somehow this seemed like a friendly continuation of an old debate. And I felt less lonely with the flickering bulb for company.

2

In Traditional Chinese Medicine, wind is often considered pernicious.
It comes in from the outside, invading the body and causing illness.
Called "the spearhead," because it opens you up to damp and cold,
wind is rarely seen as beneficent. But in Ayurveda, wind is not an out-
sider. It's instead one of the primary bhutas (the five great elements),
representing the forces of movement and change within us.

The house had become like a tree whose upper branches had died; it was silent overhead, but life still lurched along in my apartment in the roots. Or tried to lurch along. I'd been puzzling through my thesis proposal, seated at a skinny pine table I'd scored at the Chelsea Flea Market. The writing hadn't been going well. Work hadn't been going well either. Claire was only speaking to me about teaching—nothing personal—and Nathaniel, the headmaster, looked startled and weepy every time I passed him in the hall.

I thumbed through another stack of color-coded index cards, feeling jittery from sitting so long. My adviser wanted a clear thesis proposal before he left for summer break. I was pretty much out of time. I needed to quickly find a way to make the mental leap from collecting facts to having a hypothesis about those facts. Without an idea around which my paper could revolve, my master's thesis was stalled out. But I had nothing except a stack of index cards, an irritated itching in my palms and thighs, a sensation that my entire body was chanting *move, move, move.*

It was time to run.

Let's be clear: I'm not a runner. I'm not even a tiny bit athletic. I tore the ligaments and tendons in my left ankle when I was eight—in an accident involving a Shaun Cassidy poster and an old-fashioned school desk—which left me with a joint prone to rolling over and playing dead, often at the most inopportune times. Tryouts for the college crew team? Check! Three days of bed rest and the trainer explaining to me that, if I wanted to be walking at the age of forty, there could be no more running—ever.

But after a full day of teaching and avoiding Claire and an evening trying to sort the index card notes, I needed one of my rare running excursions. The full moon was beckoning, hanging low over the streetlights. As I looked out the window, I forgot my fear of a twisted ankle and threw off my otherwise healthy respect for the city's muggers.

"I'm going running!" I called to the light bulb, pulling a fleece over my yoga clothes. I waved to the bulb as I slipped out the door and onto the cobbled street. My breath already seemed less jagged, my throat no longer seemed to be closing. Tentatively I tried a deep inhale—down into the belly like we'd learned in yoga class.

Better.

Since there was no traffic, I walked down the middle of the road, rolling my neck as I lengthened my stride. The night noises from the main drag—a radio, a slammed car door—got louder as I picked up my pace and the cool air began to calm the clawing feeling inside of me. I let my breath even out, steaming in short puffs from my mouth like dragon smoke.

Under the moon, the cobbled backstreets became a fairyland: brownstones lit from within, gardens tucked up for the night behind their wrought-iron gates, the air tanged with salt and curry and the slightly burnt smell of espresso. As I ran, counting my steps—*one two three, one two three*—everything softened until I was only maybe in New York, until I was a time traveler cruising through or a will-o'-the-wisp flying by.

In Brooklyn, the tightly gridded streets and the breezes off the bay colluded to create a strange phenomenon: Even when the weather was clear, like on this cloudless night, the wind would gust down certain byways, accelerating unnaturally. If you happened to have a strong umbrella, you could get a little bit of lift—not a Mary Poppins kind of lift, but just enough that you'd feel lighter. Occasionally, when the wind was particularly strong, there would be a moment of suspension, like the pause at the apex of a horse's leap. You'd have just a second to wonder—before your feet inevitably touched the sidewalk—if this time you would stay aloft.

As I ran through the in-between of that New York City night, I called up that feeling of floating. Just thinking of it eased open a door inside my heart and my muscles recalled the lift of my feet leaving the ground for just a nanosecond longer than they should. I called to the feeling and to the wind, before taking one long airborne step, the perfume of rugosa roses swirling off my skin.

Sometimes in those rare moments under the moon's light, I felt like maybe I'd found a little magic after all.

3

Every twenty-seven to twenty-nine years, Saturn returns to its original position in your natal astrological chart, completing its romp through all twelve signs of the zodiac. When Saturn—known as the Cosmic Teacher—arrives, life will start delivering lessons whether you're ready or not. A Saturn Return is a rite of passage, a transition from one stage of life to the next, a chance to reevaluate the decisions you've made so far. Expect a reset as you revisit and revise your life's map to better suit your soul.

It was June, and it was my birthday. Twenty-nine. Jan had been gone two and a half months. My plan was to go to my parents' for the summer, then move in with another teacher for the next school year. Claire was the executor of Jan's estate, so now, in addition to being my boss, she was my landlord. It was too much; I couldn't stay.

Kneeling on the worn wooden floorboards, I smoothed the duvet, making a flat spot. Laying out a tarot spread had been my birthday ritual for a few years now. It was one of the things I'd latched onto in my ongoing quest to make life mystical.

Morning sun filtered through the window in a long wavery rectangle and gently lit the bedspread. I would miss the light here. It was a surprising thought. I remembered back to last summer and my first impressions of the place. But the old glass windows, streaked and bubbled, softened the sunshine, giving it a watery quality I'd come to love. Sometimes I stared at the panes until my eyes blurred, trying to see atoms within the glass drifting and dripping. Knowing that glass was liquid, not solid, made the centuries-old window feel alive and wise and somehow aware.

It was early, but the day was already warming. I imagined the glass was content, molting a little faster in the languid sunshine.

It would be nice to feel something as gentle as contentment.

Unbeknownst to me, my Saturn Return had begun the day before. Would it have helped to know this Cosmic Teacher and Taskmaster wreaked a bit of havoc in everyone's life? Would it have eased the burden of death and change? I'd like to think that maybe it would have given me perspective, helped me feel a little less adrift. But even inside of my mystical quest, I wouldn't have tolerated a blind belief in cosmic predestiny.

My hands shuffled the deck I'd given to myself after architecture school. I liked the sensation of it and the way shuffling gave my hands something to do, the way it made me feel a little mysterious. My eyes and mind drifted, looking for constellations in the window's glass bubbles while my hands bridged the cards. Shuffle seven times, cut into three piles—that was how I'd been taught to begin. It was a very specific formula that made no sense, but whatever: none of it really made sense. So I still followed the instructions I'd been given by a school friend. It was her deck we had used on birthdays, laying out one card for the past, one for the present, and one for the future to predict the year to come. Reading the cards was a communal activity; we worked out the meaning over wine and birthday cake. It was more a conversation starter than a divination. Using the cards when I was by myself felt different, less like a game. I lined up the card piles on the duvet cover: past on the left, present in the middle, future to the right.

Taking a sip of coffee from the mug at my knee, I flipped the top card of each pile.

Past: the Chariot, reversed.

Present: the Devil, reversed.

Future: Strength.

All three cards were Major Arcana. In my four years of working with tarot, I'd learned to pay attention when these images appeared because they represented major shifts in philosophy or fate, sometimes both.

Since I could never remember the cards' exact meanings, I paged through the tiny booklet that came with the deck.

The Chariot, reversed: riot, quarrel, litigation, defeat

The Devil, reversed: evil, weakness, pettiness, blindness

*Strength: power, energy, action, courage, complete success
   and honors*

Wow, we're not messing around this year, I thought.

Even on the smoothed bedspread, the cards weren't lying flat. The Chariot careened on two wheels, ready to take out the Devil. The past was running down the present . . . The feeling of being out of control and confronting personal demons? No news there. And pettiness? Was I being petty with Claire? Was she being petty with me?

The Strength card sat alone, slightly apart from the other two. On it, a woman had her arms wrapped around the neck of a lion. The lion seemed to be a part of her, flowing up from her depths. In the Rider-Waite-Smith deck, the woman on the Strength card conquers her fear, peering into the mouth of the lion, but in this deck, the Palladini, the image implied something else: a merging, a becoming.

I picked up the card and my coffee. Nabbing my journal from the kitchen table, I tucked it under my arm and padded barefoot out the back door. Setting everything down on the cast-iron patio table, I paced to the maple in the garden's center, the flagstones warm on my soles. Jan felt closer here. I reached out. Fire red leaves rasped against my fingertips. Tilting my face toward the sun, I closed my eyes.

"Jan?" I whispered. "I made it to twenty-nine."

The faintest breeze whispered across my cheek.

Tears pricked behind my lids.

I stood in the sun, its warmth haloing me, radiating from my head like a mane. I sent a little wish into the morning—a wish that this year I would find my strength.

4

For Heartsickness:

1 part rose petals to soften the heart
1 part hawthorn flowers to call you home
1 part mimosa flowers to remember joy
a pinch of marjoram to honor grief

Serve as tea, burn as incense, or place in a pouch under the pillow at night.

Jan's living room was dusty and cavernous. I moved through the space, touching the leaves of various plants, saying my goodbyes. The streetlights had just come on, limning the drawn velvet curtains, floor-length and lush. In a little while rush-hour traffic would be mostly past; it would be time to leave. An altered scene from an Indiana Jones movie ran its well-worn loop through my mind: me and Rosie, my Toyota Corolla, flying over the Verrazano Bridge just ahead of a giant ball of flame. Leaving New York always felt like an escape.

Down the hall, I heard a key scrape the lock of the front door.

"Shit," I murmured. The stairs down to my soon-to-be-ex-apartment were in the entryway. There was nowhere to go. I closed my eyes, head tilted toward the ceiling. I couldn't feel Jan. It was just me. I took a fortifying breath and turned. There was only one person who would be coming in at this hour.

"Hi, Claire," I called as she materialized in the dim light of the foyer. She was in a sweatshirt—unusual for her—and her hair was pulled into a gray-streaked ponytail at the base of her neck. "I just came up to say goodbye . . ." I gestured at the begonia and the painted calathea, which seemed to be leaning into our conversation. Jan had liked her plants spotted and striped.

Claire dropped her keys on the end table and walked slowly toward me. If she was angry that I was there, so be it. Her anger would wash over me. Maybe it would wash me clean.

Her hands reached up. They were small and freckled, like the paws of some forest creature. She put them on either side of my face, smiling gently into my eyes. This was the Claire I had relied on in the years before. I'd missed her.

"It's been quite a year," she said with a sad smile.

I nodded. My pain was different than hers: she had lost her closest friend, while I had lost other, less substantial, things, including her regard. I didn't have words to bridge the gap.

We stood there. The last light was fading, and a soft darkness shadowed our faces. It was likely only minutes, but in my memory that moment stretches. I remember talking, laughing a little. But I can't hear the words. My memory stutters and refuses to move on from the feel of her hands on my face, my heart cracking. When the internal film unfreezes, Claire is handing me a plant. A spotted begonia in a Roseville pot, glazed warm brown and forest green. I've since looked up the planter on a site dedicated to antique pottery. It was originally part of a pair. The set was called Sunrise/Sunset.

I clutched the begonia to my chest as I walked out of the house. When I got to the car, I nestled the plant into the passenger-seat wheel well.

I don't know what I thought at the time, putting the key into Rosie's ignition, the feel of Claire's hands still warm on my cheeks. Did I think we were mending, or did I know we had just acknowledged we were irrevocably broken? That a spider-silk strand, one of the anchors of my Brooklyn life, had just been snipped.

―――――――

Orb spiders reweave their web every night. They ingest the old strands so they can reuse the previous web's proteins. I think of this sometimes when I resist change—a spider's willingness to unweave as well as weave.

As I drove away from Jan's on that long-ago evening, I suspect I could feel the unraveling. There was a sense of unwinding at the core of my being, the free-falling sensation of a web being ingested. Still, I thought, I, or the passage of time, would spin a patch.

But after the supporting silks are snipped and the web is curled by the winds, there is no fixing things. It's time to ingest and start again. The old silks will be used to create something new. The spiral will emerge scene by scene, story by story.

Sadly, I didn't know this yet. I wasn't able to sense when it was time to ingest the threads and start afresh. I clung on through the collapse, planning to be back at the Illustrious Private School in the fall after spending the summer with my parents.

5

Many times upon a time, there was a witch.

The witch lived in the deep dark forest. . . .

The witch lived in a cottage by the sea. . . .

The witch lived in a basement apartment in Brooklyn, taught second
*   grade, and loved both sushi and mint mocha milkshakes, but not at*
*   the same time.*

As these events were transpiring in the external world, something quite different was happening in my internal realms: a dormant part of me was waking up.

Maybe it was the loneliness that sent me searching inward, that had me pressing my ear against the locked door of my subconscious, listening at the place where my inner witch muttered her musings through the keyhole. *Symbol and sign, myth and magic,* she murmured.

My ears perked up. Was there a way for the sharp fragments of my life to be reassembled into a different pattern? Could I make meaning for myself from the morass I'd been stumbling through?

My inner witch smiled knowingly and hummed a jaunty little tune.

6

To connect with your lineage:
Place one drop of blood on a chunk of dragon's blood resin. Burn.
Inhale the incense. Cup the smoke, holding it over your eyes, pulling it
over your head.
Ask your blood to speak.

It seemed that Death had followed me to my parents' home.

By the time I arrived at the hospital, Grandma was unconscious, her bulk somehow small on the bed. Flexible tubes ran this way and that, making her look like some strange sea creature captured and held in a sci-fi movie tank. Mom opened the curtains on the big window that faced the parking lot. Outside, the trees waved their shamrock-green hands, swaying a little. I wanted to sway with them, but I couldn't feel the breeze, only the air-conditioning.

Late-morning light illuminated the planes of both their faces. I wasn't used to having an angular family. Grandma had been round and loud. There's a photo of her dancing at my parents' wedding, her head thrown back and her mouth open, arm cocked exuberantly. She was in a beige satin sheath dress despite being zaftig. Mom was never big, but there had been a softness before that was gone now. I glanced over. She was looking out the window, watching a wine-colored SUV navigate a parking spot.

Last summer, she herself had been in a bed like this one, her skin mustard yellow, her breathing so quiet that more than once I'd thought she was gone. For hours, I'd hold her golden hand, listening to the doctors as they checked and rechecked her bilirubin and albumin. After sitting with Mom for a stretch, I'd run up the steps to the eighth floor, where Grandma was in a matching room. The hospital had elevators, but after sitting so long, I preferred the stairs. I can't remember what stage the lung cancer was in at that point or why, exactly, Grandma had been admitted. But I do remember the metal door that clanged as I yanked it open, the gray cement that slapped against the soles of my shoes, and the afternoon I ran into my mom's doctor on the sixth-floor landing.

"Your mom's on four," he said, trying to be helpful.

"Yeah, but my grandmother's on eight," I replied.

Above his white coat, his eyes widened almost imperceptibly. His lower face was bearded, so I couldn't see his mouth. But I knew that when it opened, I wouldn't be able to handle whatever sympathy came out. "Thanks," I said firmly, trying to make *thank you* mean *I've got this.*

Mom had recovered from her terrifying bout with hepatitis. Grandma, on the other hand, had continued to decline. Recently they'd found cancer in her hip which led to a surgery and her current hospitalization. She'd been unconscious since I arrived. Her monitors beeped gently. I noticed that none of her doctors were checking on her. I suspect they knew she was dying; there was nothing left they could do. Instead the nurses came and went, checking her vitals, changing bags of intravenous fluid. Mom got up from her chair to needlessly rearrange the blanket, tucking in my grandma's feet. With her mother's passing, Mom would be the matriarch of the family. Maiden, Mother, Crone—the shifting roles we get to play, as inevitable as the changing seasons. It was a startling thought that with the passing of my grandmother, the current crone, I too would need to shift. Maiden would become Mother. What did the word *mother* mean for me, a bisexual woman who didn't want kids? As an experiment, I put my hand low on my belly. I felt nothing: no pull, no yearning. Bearing and raising children was not my path. But one did not skip from Maiden to Crone. So what would *Mother* look like for me?

I held my grandmother's limp, feather-skinned hand, staring at the red do-not-resuscitate band clasping her wrist. That hand had reached into the glove compartment of her tan Buick sedan to pull out strawberry ropes of licorice, warm from the summer sun. She'd hand one to my sister and one to me, before chewing on one herself. "I prefer the chocolate. But I know you girls like these," she'd say. As I held her hand, my mouth moved, chewing the phantom licorice. She'd been shaking her head when we first came in—*no, no, no*—but now she was still and quiet.

Just a few days ago, the doctor had said, "The surgery went fine. Her new hip is cancer-free and strong enough for dancing!" He was optimistic, jolly with success. But soon enough the morphine they'd given her for pain began to depress her system. Her kidneys started to fail. They thought they could turn her around. They said it would be a day until we knew which way it would go.

"Let's get some lunch," Mom suggested. "Nothing's happening here."

We gathered our things. Patting Grandma's hand, I murmured, "We'll be right back."

———————

When we returned, the door to my grandmother's room was closed. An emptiness seeped from the gap between the wood laminate and the floor, an exhale I recognized from Jan's house.

Later, the nurse would tell us that sometimes a patient would wait for the family to leave before they let themselves die. My first careening thought was *if we had stayed, she would still be here.*

I'd never seen a dead person before. Now, back in the chair I'd sat in earlier, I stared at her hand, wondering if I should touch it. I remembered writing a scathing essay about her for high school English class. She'd been visiting from Florida, washing dishes at the kitchen sink. I stopped to kiss her cheek as I left for school. She looked up from the suds, assessed my outfit, and said, in her cringeworthy Philadelphia accent, "Are those chandeliers hanging from your ears?"

I wrote a revenge essay. I got an A. Sitting next to her body, I flushed with shame. Resolutely, I reached for her hand, hesitating for half a heartbeat before skin touched skin. Hers was neither warm nor cold. There was no tension in her fingers, but then there hadn't been before we'd left for lunch either. How could I think of her as gone when I was sitting right next to her?

Her monitors were silent, but I could hear the faint pings of other monitors in other rooms. The dust motes shimmering in the afternoon light seemed to bounce a little. Like an inhale. I glanced at her heart monitor. It was turned off. Still, there was movement. I was sure. I could feel it in our hands.

"Mom? Mom!" I called my mother back from her contemplation of the parking lot. "Is she breathing?"

"No," my mom said, squeezing my shoulder. "That's you. That's your breath."

———————

In the car, driving home, Mom said, "The surgery went fine; the patient died." Then she said it again. And again.

Later, sitting side by side on the soft cream sofa in my parents' tastefully pinstriped sunroom, I asked, "What do we do now?"

How had we become a family with no idea what to do in the aftermath of death? We were so very good at life. Competent. We got things done. By the age of twelve, I could navigate an airport on my own, rescuing suitcases from the baggage carousel while my dad went for the rental car. But I had no map for death. It was a landscape I kept visiting, but it remained an untamed vista without so much as a trail marker.

Intellectually, I knew that when someone died, I was supposed to feel some great and moving thing. But what I actually felt was a void, like the hole I used to stick my tongue into after a tooth fell out. It seemed small, that hole, more a thought than a feeling: *so sad they're gone.* My heart would hurt, but only a little. It was later, in a million small ways, that the absence would become truly visceral, that my heart would develop its mysterious ache. The ache would return at Thanksgiving, a holiday suddenly silent without Grandma's booming laughter, and again at Passover when Mom made hockey-puck matzah balls instead of the light, fluffy ones her mother had served up.

It took a while for these instances to accumulate, for the grief to move from my head to my heart.

That day, I sat numb on the sofa, simply looking for the next action, the next thing to do. I glanced at my mom, sitting forward on the couch, staring at her hands.

"Mom? What do we do?" I asked again, moving in closer, shoulder to shoulder. She leaned closer, reaching for my hand. I waited, ready to spring into action.

But her answer left me stranded.

"I have no idea," she replied.

7

In Jewish tradition, mirrors are covered during the period of shiva, or mourning. Some say this is so we focus on the one who has passed and not on ourselves. But there's more to this custom: reflective surfaces are scrying tools. They allow us to see, briefly, into other realms. Covering mirrors helps mourners stay in the present, in the physical world, where they are less likely to follow their loved one down the corridors of death.

We did, of course, figure out what to do after my grandmother's passing. It started simply. My mom looked up from our clasped hands and said, "Let's phone Aunt Gloria."

Aunt Gloria was not a blood relative. She was my mom's best friend. She was also Jewish in a way no one in my family managed, or desired, to be. Sure, both families belonged to the same synagogue; I went to Hebrew school with her kids. But on our side of the street, Judaism was social and political: my parents went to shul not to chat with God but to connect with their culture; they donated to United Jewish Appeal; they felt vaguely guilty when they ate shellfish or bought a car made in Germany. But for

Aunt Gloria, Judaism was the weft of her being. It enlivened and fed her spirit. It was both a compass and a map. Her blood told her exactly what to do when someone died.

> *Yit-ga-dal v'yit-ka-dash sh'mei ra-ba, b'al-ma di-v'ra chi-ru-tei, v'yam-lich mal-chu-tei.*
>
> *(Glorified and sanctified be God's great name throughout the world which He has created according to His will.)*

These first words of the Mourner's Kaddish had played through my mind in the days following Jan's death. I kept looking for comfort in the Kaddish's cadence, but the words remained dry and dusty in my mouth. But as I watched Aunt Gloria pray after my grandma's passing, it was obvious these words were not dust to her. They were rooted and grounded something vital within her being. They connected her to a lineage that knew what to do when someone died.

I joined the moving meditation that took over my parents' home. Mom's friends slid through a spontaneous choreography, touching a shoulder or nodding gently as they passed her on their way to cover mirrors and put yarmulkes in a basket by the door. The rabbi stopped in. Trays of lox and whitefish were delivered. Bags of bagels appeared. "Sit," Aunt Gloria said over and over to my mother. "You don't have to do anything."

On each of the three nights my family sat shiva, a *minion* arrived. Sometimes these were people we knew; other times they were members of the congregation doing community service: attending so we had enough people present to say the prayers for the dead. My grandmother's friends showed up with stories, their bright barks of laughter lightening the mourning.

As the congregants gathered the third night, I retreated to the screened-in porch. I'd never been able to reconcile the tenets of Judaism with my admittedly nebulous spiritual beliefs. As the sun set, fireflies began to dance on the far side of the screen. They circled the oak tree and blinked through the meadow beyond the house. Inside, there was a droning hum of voices, but on the porch, it was the katydid chorus that declared the sanctity of the night. I sat on the picnic table, facing the growing darkness.

My soon-to-be brother-in-law, dressed in sharply creased dress pants and a button-down shirt, stuck his head out the kitchen door, rousing me from my reverie.

"Are you coming in?" he asked, his voice a match for the moment with its lilting Israeli accent. "The service is starting."

Melancholy rose in my throat; claws scraped my vocal cords. I knew that what I needed wasn't in there.

I twisted to look at him. "Do you believe God is everywhere?" I asked.

"Of course," he answered. I could hear the smirk in his voice but couldn't interpret it. He'd already had more pain in his life than most could bear. His relationship with God, if there was one, was a mystery to me.

"Then if God wants me, She can find me here," I said.

David grinned. One tooth overlapped another, giving his smile a dose of added charm.

"I like the way you think," he said and winked before he ducked back into the house.

Voices rose as he opened the door; katydids took over as he closed it. The inside voices praised a god I'd never met, a demanding god who had never folded me under a wing or took the time to quiet my fears. The katydids sang the glory of the night, which every evening draped me in darkness, offering up dreams and visions and possibilities. The night held me when I cried and offered stars to dry my tears. I could picture my grandma held in the bosom of the darkness, listening as the katydids trilled their hallelujah chorus. I could meet her in that almost place, and together, we could look for shooting stars and recall the stories etched by the constellations. The foreign phrases chanted by my friends and family inside didn't conjure her. I had to unwind the words and search between their spaces for meaning and comfort. Out here, there was nothing to reconcile. I listened to the night noises and watched the stars pop out. Out here, I could just be. I didn't have to mentally modernize archaic prayers or feel like a hypocrite for speaking words I didn't believe. I didn't have to seek for a sense of spirit; it simply surrounded me.

Wind rustled my hair along with the oak's leaves. Orion's Belt brightened, and something in my chest felt lighter. Suddenly I understood: *these* were the sensations I needed from the sacred. These were the sensations my childhood religion had never offered me. For decades I'd been angry at Judaism because it hadn't shown me how to feel *this*. This sense of sanctity. Of belonging. Of peace. For decades I'd argued with the religion of my childhood, trying to wring *this* feeling out of its rituals and prayers. The need to sense myself as a part of this vastness was the burning core of my being. I wanted a clear path to it so desperately that I kept arguing. As if, once badgered enough, Judaism would give up its secrets.

Even that past year, decades after I had declared myself an atheist, I had still been fighting. It was Passover, and seder was, as usual, at Aunt Gloria's. The meal was served in the living room, where the couches were pushed closer to the TV to create space for three long folding tables set in a *U*. She never used the dining room for seder. Maybe there were simply too many of us—four Jewish families in the neighborhood and now various spouses and partners. With tablecloths, silverware, wineglasses, and whatever kitschy thing she'd chosen for decoration, the folding tables managed to feel festive. This spring she'd found tiny toy frogs. These were scattered, plague-like, around the place settings. When you squeezed the little frog belly, a vocal sac expanded under its chin. It looked like the frog was breathing: inhale, then exhale.

I sat next to Jeff, ignoring the service in favor of inflating and deflating the frog. Inhale, exhale. Jeff and I had grown up together. I knew he would point out where we were in the prayer book when, as the reading of the service circled the table, it was my turn to chime in. *Blah, blah, blah* went the readings. *Inhale, exhale* went the frog. And then we came to a special section Aunt Gloria had added a few years back. It spoke of the ancient enslavement of the Jews to Pharaoh and how it was our duty, remembered every Passover, to continue to stand up for those who were afflicted. The reading ended with a chant of *never again*.

The frog quivered in my fingers as I squeezed a little too hard. "Hypocrisy," I muttered. My mother blanched. My father, not having heard, looked at her questioningly. Aunt Gloria's older son, Mike, raised a glass and said, under his breath, "Hail Elijah!" a joke from when we were tweens. Mom whispered to Dad. He caught my eye. But Aunt Gloria was ready for me. "Say more," she suggested.

"How about we just move on? Who has the next reading?" Mom asked brightly.

"It's okay, Judy. A seder should be a discussion." Aunt Gloria looked at me expectantly.

"We're sitting here saying *never again* while there's a genocide happening in Kosovo right now. It's hypocritical." I glared around the room.

You would think the table would have sunk into stunned silence, but these people had known me my whole life. At least one interruption was expected. Surreptitiously, Ed, whom I'd known since I was five, checked his watch under the table. My lips twitched.

"Ah!" Aunt Gloria exclaimed. "You always bring up the best points for discussion!"

Mom closed her eyes and put her head in her hands.

I look back at that seder now and see that beneath the anger, there was a searching. A seeking for threads of connection and the webbing that binds the world of spirit with material reality. *How do we connect to the suffering of other people? What is the path to the place where we are all one? How do we infuse our words, our prayers, with meaning and purpose and action?*

In Judaism there's a concept called *tikkun olam*. It's often simply translated as "charity." But it's more nuanced than that. *Tikkun* means "to repair." *Olam* means "the world." It is our duty not simply to give to charity, but to repair the world. To repair this beautiful, broken place we call home, this orbiting satellite of the sun, careening through the night sky.

It's in moments like this, when linguistic layers of meaning are exposed, that I love the religion of my people. There is a depth of understanding that exists right alongside the archaic prayers to a patriarchal god. The world is broken, and it is up to each of us to offer what healing we can. The web is tangled; it's up to us to respin it.

Inside the house, I could hear the front door opening and closing as mourners departed. Aunt Gloria's salt-and-pepper head was bent over the kitchen sink. Next to her on the counter, the shiva candle flickered. I didn't think I could ever view Judaism the way that Aunt Gloria did, but over the years, it had become increasingly obvious that she was tapped into something the rest of us weren't. Trust, faith, devotion, generosity, kindness, knowing what to fight for—she seemed to understand, not with her mind but with her heart, what the next right action needed to be. She seemed to live *tikkun olam*.

I couldn't put faith in the god of the Old Testament, but was there another path to Aunt Gloria's grounded surety? To her fiery compassion? Could I somehow become as solid and integral to the world as she was? As I watched her orchestrating the mourning days after my grandma died, I'd begun to realize that I had ripped Judaism out of my life without replacing it. My inner worlds lacked a structure for the sacred. I could stumble upon it randomly on a starlit night on the porch but I had no map or compass to guide me there intentionally. I knew no prayer to open that door.

Maybe it was time to ingest the proteins and spin new threads, to craft a web of my own design instead of simply trashing the one I'd inherited. To do so, I would need to find a reliable way to connect with something greater than myself. I would need replicable rituals that let me add my stitches to the work of repairing the world.

I thought about sewing. Before I stitched a rip, I chose my needle—short and sharp or long and wide. Each needle did slightly different work. Then I matched my thread, or didn't, if I wanted to create contrast. It was only after threading the needle that I examined the rip, choosing where to begin, deciding the type of stitch required.

I didn't know how to repair the world, but maybe I could start by restitching my *self.* As I looked inward, it was obvious I didn't know how to do that either. But I could choose my tools.

Tilting my chin up to the stars, I opened my ears to the katydid choir, and allowed the word *hello* to whisper across my tongue. In response came an upwelling of warmth and a word, a meaning, vibrating in my heart: *welcome.*

8

There are many types of memory. Rosemary stimulates the memory of the mind: crush it between your fingers and inhale. But the body has its own memories, memories tucked in the interstitial spaces that rosemary cannot reach. Yarrow travels the blood, awakening muscle memory. Motherwort wafts through dream time, calling to the soul. And frankincense? Frankincense rides the links of lineage, connecting you to your past's past.

"I've never seen this one before," I said, passing a sepia photo to my mom. The late-August light was creeping across the sunroom's warm wood floors. Soon I would return to Brooklyn. I'd been keeping my mom company as she did the myriad tasks that followed Grandma's death—the trips to Goodwill, the bank, the notary. My presence was for her sake but also for my own. "What is it like to lose a mother?" I remember asking her. She was sorting mail at the kitchen counter. I can see her flipping through the envelopes, but I can't remember how she answered. I was acutely aware that the loss she was feeling—that of a daughter losing a mother—would someday be my own.

Mom took the photo from me and flipped it over. On the back, in slanting script, was my grandmother's maiden name: *Sarah Lam.*

"I don't remember it either," Mom said, handing it back to me. We had made tea and taken it into the sunroom, plunking down on the same striped love seat we'd sat on when we returned from the hospital. Photos of Grandma were spread on the coffee table. We were trying to organize them but it was hopeless: we just kept sifting through, sharing memories and telling stories.

I examined the red-browns of the mystery photo. The young woman in it had a scarf tied round her head, rouged lips, a coy smile, and a violin tucked under her chin.

"Did Grandma play the violin?" I asked, trying to reconcile the fiery figure—a woman who could obviously charm a sultan or pull off a bank heist—with the person I called "grandma." How many lives do we experience in one lifetime? How often do we go into the cocoon, shed one skin, and emerge as someone else? Sometimes I think this constant becoming is the essence of reincarnation—with each transformation we are more and more refined, more and more ourselves. But maybe, I realized looking at the photo, we lose something, too. Mom reached over and took the picture back, studying it.

"I think she played. When she was young," Mom said slowly. She reached for her tea mug, sipping as she thought about it. "She worked all the time after my father died. First she had a luncheonette, then a dress shop." The implication was clear: there was no time for music.

Yet the violin rested easily under my grandma's chin. Her gaze was direct and cocky, her posture one I recognized from my sister's childhood practice sessions—violin on the shoulder, bow at the ready. But there was something in my grandmother's stance, something brash and direct, that I'd never seen in my sister. What gets passed down epigenetically? Where did violin playing sit in my genetic lineage? Where did brashness? Why didn't I inherit either?

Over dinner many years ago, Grandma had intervened when my sister was ribbing me: *You must be the milkman's daughter; you don't like **anything** the rest of us like!* Grandma had glared, blue eyes wide. "You think no one else in this family likes horses? When I was your age, I would take my father's horse from the ice cart when he came home for lunch. I rode bareback," she added proudly, winking at me. The rest of the family gaped.

There are no photos of my grandma riding, but in my mind, her flaxen hair streams down her back and her chin juts stubbornly. A young goddess, both wild and caged.

———————

Horses are the same way—both caged and wild. We forget they're prey animals. Most flinch at loud noises and shy from quick movements. To be safe around them, you must turn yourself into steady ground so that your calm transcends their natural fear.

But what happens when you can't?

In my mind, my inner eight-year-old laces up her riding boots, getting ready to go to the barn. By the time the boots were tied, panic would have been pushing up against her diaphragm, making it hard to breathe.

This gnawing terror became predictable. As my mom backed down the driveway, turning the car away from the suburban houses and toward the farm fields and pastures, I'd begin to get nauseous. I still don't know what made my younger self approach this churning breathless place week after week. I can't say why, at twelve, my life still revolved around the polestars of love and fear. Looking back, you'd think at some point I would have sighed with relief when my mom asked if she should turn the car around. I can hear her saying, "You don't have to do this," her tone confused and exasperated. And yet, despite trainer after trainer pulling her aside and whispering that they'd never seen a child so terrified, she continued to take me to the stables. And despite the queasy breathlessness, I continued to insist upon going. There was something I was learning, someone I was becoming, and horses were helping me do it.

In homeopathic medicine, there's a principle: *like treats like.* So to treat poison ivy, for instance, you take a miniscule amount of homeopathic poison ivy. I was a scared kid, which is not surprising: anxiety runs through my family lines. Perhaps snuggling up with a prey animal—itself trying to learn how to be strong, focused, and fearless in this human world—was a form of homeopathic medicine.

Often, I hear people talk about spirit animals or familiars in the abstract. They vie to be partnered with a sexy leopard or a farseeing hawk, wanting the animal they identify with to reflect their most elevated aspects. But maybe what we really need is to learn from the animals who reflect our soft and tender places, our perceived deficits, the parts of ourselves we need to evolve to survive this world.

After a decade of riding terrified, the shift came in a flash. I was fourteen and my parents had decided to buy me a horse of my own. My trainer and I had been visiting various stables, trying a multiplicity of horses. Too big, too small, too old, too young, too lame, too headstrong.

One afternoon in early spring, the ground heavy with snowmelt and the trees barely budding, we'd driven out to see a bay mare. She was the right age and height, sound, and purported to be sane. When we pulled into the gravel lot next to the riding ring, we saw the horse's trainer had her saddled and ready to go. The mare was dancing in circles, jerking her head against the reins. Rich, my trainer, got out of the truck and stood watching for a moment.

"This one's not for you," he said through the rolled-down window. "Give me a minute, and we'll get out of here." He headed over to speak with the other trainer.

I got out of the cab. Rich, in his tweed flat cap, towered over the other man as they conversed. Rich gestured toward me. The shorter man nodded. They both looked so casual, so relaxed. The horse jiggered. Rich's hands were now in the pockets of his barn coat. He didn't flinch as the horse shied and almost stepped on his foot. Instead, he just leaned with his shoulder, pushing her away. My insides went gooey, and my breath came fast.

And so I did the brave thing: I opened the door of the truck and grabbed my chaps. Focusing on the leather, I managed the buckle at the waist and the long zippers up my legs, while I tried to get control of my fear. Reaching back into the cab, I fished my helmet out of the wheel well and walked to the ring.

Chutzpah, my grandma would have called it.

Rich watched me come, assessing. "This is not the right horse for you," he called, in his most calm and reasonable tone—a tone he used with me often. "It's okay. You don't have to ride her. You don't have to do this."

But I did. I moved up next to the mare, putting one hand on the saddle's pommel and bending my left leg at the knee. Rich didn't argue. He stepped closer. I held my leg stiff as he grasped my knee and ankle, levering me onto the mare's back.

"Five minutes," he said, helping me adjust the stirrup leathers as the horse quivered and sidestepped.

Shoulders stiff, breath tight, I headed to the rail. The horse shimmied beneath me. We both huffed nervously. We both squirmed in discomfort. And suddenly, just like that, I saw, not her, but *myself*. I saw her reflecting me back to me.

"It's okay," I told her, stroking her neck. "We can do this. It's okay."

And I meant it. It was okay. I was okay; she was okay. Applying a little leg pressure, I moved her into a trot.

———————

Rosie the Corolla was packed and ready for the drive back to Brooklyn. I planned to leave the next morning, after the morning rush hour. There was one more Grandma-related task to do that afternoon and, in the evening, we had reservations at my parents' favorite Italian restaurant, a tiny bistro just down the street. And then summer would be officially over. It was time to return to the Illustrious Private School.

I paced the lobby as Mom fished in her purse for the tiny manilla envelope that held the safe-deposit-box key. The bank manager joined her, his key in hand, and they processed to the vault where Mom would lay to rest Grandma's jewelry: a pear-shaped diamond—an engagement gift from her second husband—and the ruby-bedecked butterfly pin my mom had given Grandma on her eightieth birthday. I could see Mom through the open vault door, the metal safe-deposit box laid out on a counter-height table. She was removing papers, inspecting each document. In the overly air-conditioned lobby, I rubbed at my goose-bumped arms. All I could see was the top of Mom's head as she continued to sift through the papers. She rarely went into the box; there were probably decades of now-useless ephemera in there. I shivered again. The bank tellers were in summer suits, their long sleeves offering protection from the frigid air. Beyond the glass double entry doors, the shimmering heat of the parking lot beckoned, suddenly appealing.

"I'll be right outside," I murmured to the bank manager, making my escape before my teeth began to chatter.

On the walkway, I paused to let my skin soak up the blissful warmth. It was still summer, but the oppression had lifted; autumn waited in the wings, ready to make her entrance. There were daisy-like Helenium fronting the foundation shrubbery, and while I couldn't smell them over the gasoline scent wafting from the service station next door, the bees obviously could. They were humming happily amidst the flowers when a butterfly—black wings brushed with startling blue—fluttered in to join them.

I'd seen countless butterflies since Grandma had died. They hovered in the front garden and appeared on the sympathy cards that were still sprinkled in with my parents' mail. I saw them on books and T-shirts. A friend's shower curtain. A refrigerator magnet. My grandmother had hung metal butterflies on the wall of her Florida sunroom, their wings painted seventies ocher and burnt orange. They were a secret sign of metamorphosis hidden in plain sight.

Family myth says *horsy* was the first word out of my mouth, as if I'd learned language simply to make that one all-important pronouncement. I wonder sometimes what animal burbled in the back of my grandmother's psyche when, as a baby, she first experimented with *da* and *ba*. Was *horse* what spoke to her soul or was riding her father's ice-cart gelding the equivalent of stealing the car keys and going for a spin?

Watching the blue-and-black wings flutter, I suspected her animal was butterfly. Each time I saw one, it felt like a kiss on the forehead. In some odd way, they were like the flickering light bulb at Jan's house: *I'm not gone, just transformed*, they seemed to say. *It's all connected. We're all connected,* their wings seemed to whisper.

And then, more quietly, so it was just a single note vibrating within my heart, I sensed the word that had come to me as I sat under the stars listening to the katydids:

Welcome.

9

To release the energy of the past, imagine that you can gather it in your hands. Pluck it out of your heart and your hair; let it rise from your lungs so that it can travel down your arms. Collect it from the world around you, yanking back the stories you've told, reeling them in like fish on a line.

When you have all the pieces of the past that you can carry, when they are filling your arms to overflowing, pack them into a sphere. See them in your mind, glittering like a snowball. Now give all that energy back: Drop it in the fire. Compost it in the earth. Or rinse it down the drain, knowing the water will find its way to sea, to source, and all will be cleansed.

After the excess of family time over the summer, September was a beacon. Don't get me wrong: I love my family. But there have been times throughout my life when being with them is hard work. I'm sure they'd say the same of living with me.

The summer of 1998 ranked medium-high on the difficulty meter—my sister was getting married, and the gender of my plus-one for the wedding (an unknown, since I had yet to invite a date) was causing tension. It had been a relief to pack up Rosie and head back to New York City. I unloaded at my new apartment: a two bedroom I was sharing with another teacher. It wasn't glamorous—the Brooklyn-Queens Expressway frothed right outside the kitchen window—but it was drama-free. In my mind, I had a clean slate. I was looking forward to meeting my rising second graders.

On the first day of school, I paused on the sidewalk, staring up at the stony Gothic facade. A clositer-like breezeway protected the closed doors keeping the air-conditioning in and the parents out. They mingled on the sidewalk, drinking coffee and catching up. As I eased my way through the crowd, I heard variations of *"hard to be back"* paired with destinations like *Paris, Newport,* and *the Vineyard.*

The cacophony rose as I stepped inside, voices echoing off the marble floor. A golden-haired boy in bell-bottoms, his curly hair gelled straight up and a boa around his neck, was hugging a waiflike girl in a pencil skirt and heels, her long hair brushing the shoulders of a silky bomber jacket. Both, I think, had starred in last year's spring play. I squared my shoulders and headed for the sweeping central staircase. The russet-and-gold Aubusson carpet that generously covered its width implied that this was not so much a school as a Parisian grand salon. Students mingled along its length, chattering excitedly. As I mounted the first step, the receptionist at the front desk gave me a sympathetic half wave. I smiled and waved back before entering the obstacle course of backpacks and coffee mugs.

Nathaniel stood at the first landing, where you could view the entirety of the foyer below. His gnarled fingers rested on the walnut railing, which had been polished by decades of hands grasping and butts leaning. Now in his seventies, Nathaniel had founded the school in the hopes of creating a noninstitution to nurture the artistic and contrarian. His vision had been gloriously realized, and there was more than one movie star, a top-ranked photographer, and a few authors amongst the parents in the coffee klatch outside. With his gray goatee, mock turtleneck, and rounded glasses, Nathaniel emanated satisfaction as he played out the cliché of the erudite headmaster.

"Nathaniel," I murmured as I made my way across the landing. His long gaze contracted as he turned to me. The satisfaction left his smile, and for the briefest moment he was wild-eyed and sad, bereft even. It seemed I still reminded him of Jan, and even all these months later, that was painful for both of us. His eyes were far away, not focused on me, so I continued up the steps, the still somewhat mysterious events of the spring now draped around my shoulders like a cloak. So much for a clean slate.

My classroom was on the fifth floor. My hands shook a little as I inserted the key into the lock. Lower School drop-off was later than High School so I still had a few minutes before I had to plaster a smile on my face for the new parents. *Inhale, exhale,* I schooled myself, tucking my bag into the closet. The room was prepped—I'd been working steadily for the past two weeks, decorating the walls with a ridiculous number of construction paper butterflies, laying matching name tags on the five round tables where the kids usually worked, and organizing the library, which now sported my entire childhood collection of Nancy Drew mysteries. Luckily, I'd thought to buy tissues. (Parents always needed them on first day drop-off.) I pulled one out of the paisley printed box.

The doorknob jiggled and Hallie walked in.

"Ready?" she asked as she deposited an extra-large coffee cup on our shared table and stripped off her leather jacket, dropping it on a chair. Underneath she wore a tight-fitting tank top and yoga pants.

"I just ran into Nathaniel on the stairs," I said. I sat down at the table and stole a sip of her latte. "I don't know how much longer I can do this, Hal. I thought this year would be different. Better."

"It might be; it might not be," Hallie said with her usual Confucian surety. "It's too soon to know. Have you seen Claire?"

49

"I've been avoiding the office." I reached for Hallie's latte again, and she pushed it toward me. "We had a moment the night I moved out. But I don't think it changed anything. I don't get it, Hal. I don't understand why she's so angry with me."

"When people are in pain, they don't always make sense, Em."

I got that. Claire was part of a world that no longer made sense. When I'd started at the school, she was the surrogate mom I desperately needed. Her acceptance had let me relax for the first time in years and I'd begun to think of this wacky place as home. I'd even pictured myself hanging around long enough to become a relic, like Agnes who ran the library. But now there was a squirming in my stomach: my inner-guidance system was coming online and it was warning that the situation had shifted.

10

Your Sun sign represents your outward-facing self. The way you move through the world.

Your Moon sign represents your inner self. The way you internalize the world.

Think of your Rising sign as the mask you wear or the clothes you choose to don. It's how you appear to those who don't know you well . . . and to yourself, if you haven't explored the depths of your own psyche.

P. D. Eastman wrote a popular children's book called *Are You My Mother?*, which features a baby bird wandering about, asking the all-important question featured in the title. The bird asks everything from a kitten to a car, "Are you my mother?" What the hatchling is really asking is: *Am I like you? Do I belong here?*

During the autumn of 1998, I was that baby bird. Sensing I'd been kicked out of the nest of the Illustrious Private School, I began searching out other social circles. Mike, Aunt Gloria's son (of *hail Elijah!* fame), started a dinner club; once a month, eight of us would gather in his Gramercy apartment to cook together. Friendships grown cold since my breakup were renewed—it seemed enough time had gone by that people were now willing to be both of our friends—and I started going out to hear live music again. Additionally, I began wandering the classes and weekend workshops of New York City, searching for my people. *Am I like you?* I would wonder, glancing surreptitiously around the yoga studio while stretching into downward dog. *Do I belong here?* I would ask myself as I walked across the NYU campus on my way to a meeting with my thesis adviser.

So maybe it's not surprising that I ended up in a "holistic health" class that wasn't really a holistic health class.

Why, you might be wondering, was I interested in holistic health in the first place?

The previous year, during my first semester working at the Illustrious Private School, I'd gotten sick and Western medicine had failed to find a cure . . . or even a diagnosis. The walk to work had suddenly become exhausting. I'd drag myself up the central staircase, clammy and breathless, forcing my leg to lift one more time, then one more. A creeping rash started behind my knees and slowly crawled up my body.

My doctor had run test after test. Standing at the counter in her exam room, she pushed a frizzy curl behind her ear as she reread my medical chart. "I can see you're sick. You *look* exhausted." Her half smile was an apology; who wants to be told they look exhausted? I remember her stroking my chart as though it might reveal the answer to her fingertips. Then she put it down and took an audible breath. "Western medicine isn't going to fix this," she said.

I must have looked alarmed. She hustled on. "I'm studying Traditional Chinese Medicine. I don't know much yet, but medical systems approach patterns of disease differently. Western medicine doesn't understand the pattern of your symptoms, but another type of medicine might."

My brain whirred. *Another type of medicine? There were other types of medicine?* Or maybe I should rephrase: there were other types of medicine that my doctor thought were worth considering?

So began a series of appointments with practitioners in basement offices on the Lower East Side and on living room couches in Williamsburg (long before either Williamsburg or its sofas were trendy). I learned about homeopathy and acupuncture and herbalism. I drank disgusting teas and sucked on tiny pills placed (without touching them—never touch them!) directly under my tongue.

Unbeknownst to me I was taking the first step on the path that would eventually lead me to the magic I'd been so earnestly seeking.

One afternoon, five weeks into my crash course in alternative healing, I caught the subway after work and got off at 28th Street. A few blocks up and a few blocks over, I walked down steps into an unremarkable garden apartment. The slight man behind the desk reached over, shook my hand, and pointed me toward a chair. I went through my well-rehearsed list of symptoms. He had me lick a piece of paper, which he fed into an ancient army-gray machine. A few minutes later, he gave me both his diagnosis and prescription: Candida overgrowth, eat nothing but vegetables with a little lean meat. Come back in three months.

"Can I have dressing with my salad?" I asked, trying to wrap my head around *only vegetables*.

"Salad, no dressing," he replied. "You can use olive oil." He made it sound like a huge concession.

"Can I put milk in my coffee?"

"No dairy. And no sweeteners."

"So, like, what about Chinese food?" I often got takeout from a place a few blocks from my apartment. I'd go right after school, when I could still get the lunch special, which was half the price of the dinner entrées.

"You can get steamed vegetables," he told me. "No sauce."

I stared at him in horror. "No rice?" I asked.

"No grains at all," he said grimly.

This was clearly nuts. Unfortunately, I was also clearly desperate.

Let me assure you that doing a diet like this for three months will allevi-
ate all manner of symptoms, regardless of the diagnosis. After two weeks
of these austerity measures, I was, miraculously, mostly myself again. Then
began the slow procedure of adding foods back in, noting my reactions, and
eliminating anything that caused an issue. Six months after walking down
the steps into the homeopath's basement apartment, I was no longer eating wheat, spelt, barley, or rye. A dozen years later, I recognized that this
diet—designed through trial and error—was the same as the trendy, "new"
gluten-free diet.

Growing up, I was taught that when you were sick, you went to the doctor.
But the process I had been going through encouraged me to be proactive, to
get to know my own body, to learn through experiment and experience. This
changed my foundational beliefs about wellness. It made me curious about
alternative healing, which felt vaguely like the magic I'd been seeking but also a
bit like science, albeit a secret science most people didn't acknowledge.

I began hanging out in the supplements' aisle at Perelandra Natural
Foods. Under the fluorescent lights, I'd compare the stuff on the shelves to
the write-ups in *Prescription for Nutritional Healing*. This was the nineties;
Whole Foods was just beginning its quest for world domination. The thought
that organics could be sexy and upscale was still a decade away . . . which
meant it was easy to stand in the wellness section of the nearly empty store
for hours at a time without bothering anyone.

And that brings us to the "holistic health" class, which turned out to
be more focused on astrology than anything else. If anyone had asked me—
which they didn't—I would have renamed it Astrology for Everyday Wellness.

My thoughts about astrology at the start of class went something
like this:

- Approximately one-twelfth of the population of the world are Geminis, like me. Am I supposed to believe we're all airy-fairy social butterflies? That sounds ridiculous. Plus, I'm not an airy-fairy social butterfly!
- Horoscopes give broad, general descriptions, and your mind fills in the blanks, making something that's actually generic seem specific and meaningful to you.
- I love Rob Brezsny's horoscopes; they're the first thing I flip to when I open the *Village Voice*.
- (So maybe I am a Gemini because, given everything else I believe, that's airy-fairy irrational.)

Enter the "holistic health" class.

On Tuesday night, nine of us crammed into a Chelsea apartment, sitting on floor pillows and doubled up on the couch, with a few people perched on the squared-off back. I was perched. I'd learned in past weeks that having someone sit behind me, their foot touching my hip, their knee skimming my neck as they turned to talk, was distracting—especially if that someone was the adult sex-ed teacher with the piercings and spiky bleached hair.

Our teacher, bedecked in a gold-and-purple caftan, was talking about how Pluto, planet of the underworld, was out of retrograde, but Saturn and Jupiter were still moving backward. The trines and squares and stelliums were sliding off my frontal cortex in much the same way calculus had slithered away when I was in architecture school. Ms. Spiked and Bleachy was layering on the innuendo, something about the Divine Feminine and embracing Kali and a long black tongue running up the ridge of your spine. Everyone was laughing.

Except me. I was growing increasingly uncomfortable. The apartment was too small and these women too loud, too physical.

I flashed back to a summer studying in Rome, when I had walked in on my suite mates dancing, shirts off, shimmying, touching themselves. "I love my body," one of them had purred, circling me. I stood very still, eyeing the door. I've seen horses do this—planting their feet and rolling their eyes. It obviously wasn't the reaction she was going for. My roommate huffed and put her hands on her hips. "You even sleep like you're dead," she said in disgust, closing her eyes, making her face still, and crossing her arms over her chest to mimic what was, apparently, my nighttime mien.

It was probably true. I often didn't know what to do with my body. It felt separate, somehow—not *me*. It was as though what I thought of as *I* was made from something very different than flesh. Years later, a psychic would say upon meeting me, "How do you fit in there? Your spirit is so big and amorphous! Is it strange to be in such a tiny, structured body?"

It was an odd comment, too "woo-woo" for my sensibilities, and yet it resonated. *How did I fit into a body? How do any of us fit into a body? Does it ever get comfortable?*

My mind toggled back to the present as someone slipped a box from the Donut Pub onto the coffee table. Saliva filled my mouth. I wished this were a real holistic health class and that someone could tell me what herb or homeopathic to take so I could have just one doughnut hole.

Ms. Spiked and Bleachy "accidentally" brushed my calf with her breast as she leaned forward to snag a doughnut. She sat back between my legs and smiled up at me. "So uptight, Em! It's tough with all that Earth in your chart." She licked the icing off her doughnut and flashed a pixie grin in my direction.

"All that Earth in my chart" was the revelation of the holistic health class. Turns out, we're not just our Sun signs. We have a whole astrological chart—a snapshot of the heavens at the moment of our birth. Each of our charts is as unique as a thumbprint, not generic like a Sun sign horoscope.

Turns out Ms. Spiked and Bleachy was a *triple Scorpio*: her Sun, Moon, and Rising sign all cohabitating in the watery depths. That pretty much means she was predestined to suggestively lick the icing off her doughnut holes.

What was I predestined for? Did I believe in predestiny?

More questions to ponder when I should have been working on my master's thesis.

In the epic stories I loved, characters had a purpose, a mission, a destiny. It gave their lives meaning. I wanted that—a *calling*. I thought it was a component of the magic I was searching for.

Yet the idea of predestiny—that my fate was "written in the stars"—rankled my sense of independence. Could you have both destiny and free will?

While I gnawed on this over the eight weeks of the course, I noticed something else happening: my sense of self was expanding. Learning the nuances of my chart seemed to be stretching my internal landscape. I began to see the layered aspects of my personality and felt better able to contextualize my contradictions. The perfectionism? That's Virgo. Sure it doesn't match seamlessly with the devil-may-care of my Gemini Sun, and that's okay.

I can be both.

Maybe I was born to be both.

Somewhere in the depths of my mind, a little mouse gnawed through plastic and copper, allowing old associations to fall away and new connections to form.

11

The final pose, or asana, in a modern yoga class is called savasana, a Sanskrit word which translates as "corpse pose." This is thought to be the hardest pose in yoga. It's easy to believe we're accomplishing something when we're stretching and bending; it's harder to understand that we're achieving something equally important by relaxing and letting go.

My yoga mat was blue. The room had mirrors along one wall like the ballet studio I'd danced at as a child. *So uncoordinated!* And, apparently, I'd had a "sickle point." I can still feel the ballet teacher's ruler slapping my arch.

Turns out, I was still awkward. When the yoga teacher said left, I went right. *Do I correct myself or just continue to go opposite of everyone else?* I wondered at my first yoga class. Two years later, I was still wondering the same thing, feeling turned about from everyone else in the room.

It was a relief when we lay down for savasana. My eyes closed. A thickly woven throw was draped over my body. I could feel the teacher walking the room, her quick touch on my shoulders as she passed. A low gong reverberated through my core.

"You have done everything you will do," she intoned. "Whatever was not done will remain undone."

Tears dripped from under my closed eyelids. *Whatever was not done will remain undone.* The grief rose up suddenly, more visceral now than when Jan and Grandma had died. It was like I was preserving sorrow in some internal root cellar, drying and pickling it for future use. Sometimes I'd have nightmares. Mom, who was trained as a family therapist, suggested I pause before bed to envision a superpower I could use in my dreams—like a cloak of invisibility or a potion that changed everything into flowers—that way I'd have a weapon when the dream monsters appeared.

When, I wondered, *would everything stop reminding me of death?*

And why did I still feel like a ghost? Like I was witnessing, but not a part of, the world around me?

Maybe, my psyche answered, *you are in the middle of your own metaphoric death.*

But I was still unwilling to acknowledge the ramifications of my fallout with Claire. And, if yoga unlocked the root cellar door, my subconscious decided, then maybe I should avoid yoga for a while.

12

If you lose your way, carve the four compass points onto a pillar candle (top or sides, it doesn't matter). On the night of the new moon, set the intention to find your path and purpose. Light the candle, letting it burn all the way down. Note that this is the beginning of a process; you can set a spell in motion, but you can't control the timing.

I'd always figured my future self would write a novel (best-selling, of course). But while I'd started many manuscripts, I was never gripped by a plot or compelled by a character.

For years my father had hounded me:

"When are you going to write your book?" he'd ask.

"As soon as I know the story!" I'd reply (sometimes brightly, as if to say *duh, Dad*; other times I'd grumble, my tone a clear *No Trespassing* sign).

The conversations were bubbling in the background when I saw a flier for a screenwriting workshop tacked to the bulletin board at St. Mark's bookshop. I thought, *Maybe instead of a book, I'll write a screenplay!*

That was November's passing fancy.

Plus, *my* people weren't in astrology class, and I was avoiding yoga so, in true *Are-You-My-Mother* fashion, I continued searching for a place where I might belong.

The screenwriting class was held over a long weekend in an auditorium at FIT—the Fashion Institute of Technology. In a city that loved naming its neighborhoods, FIT's location was liminal space. It was not quite Midtown and, with its drab and functional forties architecture, it certainly didn't feel like Chelsea. In lime green and sparkle, platform boots and Doc Martens, glittering constellations of students shone bright against the gray. I was intimidated by their confidence, their willingness to say *look at me!*

Finishing my coffee outside the lecture hall, I studied a shopfront display of undergrad work: bright, modern, and cutting. I felt more akin to the forties concrete. How was it that three years into living in New York I still didn't belong to Manhattan? In the plateglass window, I sized up my reflection: hair coiffed in a super-short pixie, lips plum and plumped; black pants, cropped and flared, over a pair of square-toed go-go boots. I *looked* New York. And I'd finally stopped confusing the avenues with the streets. I knew to buy my subway card from the machine instead of waiting in line at the booth with the tourists. But while I might pass on the outside, I still felt all wrong on the inside.

You can do this, I coached myself, standing a bit straighter. Tugging a tiny curl back into place, I took a deep breath and headed inside.

A spotlight lit the empty stage. Staying toward the back of the auditorium, I settled into a seat. Its springs were wonky, tilting it downward, so I scooted to the next one. Not much better. But then a man in a navy sports coat strode across the stage to the podium. Even from the nosebleed section, I could see his eyebrows were remarkable. He wriggled them a little, as if he knew their worth. Behind him the workshop title appeared in huge letters on the screen—*Story: Style, Structure, Substance and the Principals of Screenwriting*. I scrambled for my bag, found a notebook and pen, began scribbling. ... And didn't stop for three days.

59

At the end of the weekend, right hand cramped and notebook crammed, I stood with the others, tears burning my eyes as we gave Robert McKee a standing ovation. He'd just finished a lecture on the difference between being and becoming. In my notes, I had written: *Being is the honor, the value, you hold within. It is a constant. It shapes your becoming. Becoming is flux, the changes that happen in your outer life. Being is eternal, private. Becoming is external, public.*

As I stood, clapping my hands together till they stung, I imagined McKee accompanying me from the lecture hall, gesticulating with his left hand as his right reached for my shoulder. *There's a difference between your inner self, your eternal self, and the dramas of everyday life. Your being—the eternal part of you—is not stupid, or outcast, or broken, Em.*

I walked out of the lecture hall alone, dazed and somehow reborn.

Heading to the subway after class that day, the city felt . . . *different.* A little brighter, a bit more alive. Like Manhattan was a character in my story, sometimes a mentor or gatekeeper, other times a trickster or challenger, and that was *okay.* Those three days of lectures had made me realize my life was an adventure in process and that the rough spots were opportunities, not referenda. Looking west across 23rd Street, I smiled at the seal-colored gleam of the Hudson River before turning down 7th Avenue, suddenly eager for more of a walk. I found my flow in the foot traffic, feeling for the cosmic composition within the crowd's seemingly random movements.

The streets shifted to the diagonal grid that marked the entrance to Greenwich Village. On the horizon, the Twin Towers rose like pillar candles. They seemed just a few blocks away, but I knew—from blisters and experience—their nearness was an illusion. When I had first arrived in New York City, I'd worked as a temp at a financial firm in the South Tower. Feeding tax audits—page by monotonous page—into the Xerox machine, I became obsessed with the thought that architecture school had been my big chance. Like my life was a question with only one correct answer ... and I'd blown it: I'd be fetching coffee and making copies until I faded into grayness.

But with time and distance, I could see that temping was not *The End*. And neither, I realized, was Claire or the Illustrious Private School. I was still in the opening act of a life journey with all its attendant ups and downs. Thinking like a screenwriter, I could begin to see where I was in the arc of a tale that had started long ago, lying in bed at overnight camp, listening to stories about magic.

Deep in my being, a light bulb flickered, and a strand of spider silk unfurled. Jan leaned over the banister and gave me a gentle smile before heading up the stairs.

13

When new beginnings beckon, carry a moonstone in your pocket. Moonstone can help you find peace and clarity as you reinvent yourself and reorient your life. Also? It makes a great worry stone when anxiety threatens, as it inevitably will when change is afoot.

The pointed wooden doors were adorned with wreaths. Grabbing the heavy brass handle, I shouldered my way out of the wind and was rewarded with the warm scent of gingerbread. In the school's foyer, a large fir tree was decorated with ornaments the first graders had made. An electric menorah was lit on Ruth's desk. Garlands wove up the banister of the rust-and-gold-carpeted grand staircase. The upper schoolers sat on the steps in triples and pairs, dressed in glitter and faux fur, velvet and combat boots.

As usual during events, Nathaniel stood on the first landing. He was in wool tweed with a crimson bow tie, holding a glass of something that looked alcoholic.

"Happy holidays, Nathaniel," I said, raising an eyebrow as I looked at him over the top of my glasses, an affectation I was testing in the hopes of looking less like Jan. He raised his tumbler with a wistful smile before turning back to the festive scene below. I sighed and pushed the obviously useless glasses up onto my head.

It was the final evening before winter break. The Lower School parents had been invited to join their kids for a holiday celebration. Our classroom was prepped—Hallie and I had hung the kids' art and stories and laid out piles of schoolwork, a mound for each of our eighteen students. When I walked in, Hallie had a Joni Mitchell CD playing. She was straightening chairs and singing along:

But it don't snow here, it stays pretty green
I'm gonna make a lot of money and quit this crazy scene.

"I just ran into Nathaniel," I said as I shrugged out of my own vintage faux fur, dumped my bag onto a chair, and then, more carefully, I deposited a plate of cookies on the table.

"And?" Hallie asked.

"And . . . " I took a deep breath. "I can't do this anymore."

———————

Turns out, I could do it a little while longer: I made it through the school year.

Looking back on this time in my life, I see an internal pattern I've learned to recognize: In the chaos and tumult of an ending, I become desperate. The anchor silks are cut, and the web is floating free. I try to grab it, to put it back, or, when that fails, to replace it as quickly as possible.

But now I also know that in those same moments something new is beginning. The new web is still too small to recognize—is it a three-legged stool? A child's sketch of a snowflake?

I try, now, to trust my way through those moments. If I can ingest the proteins of the old weaving, I always find that the next spiral has already begun.

Coda

After the children have curled around themselves in sleep
I slip to the quiet streets below
breathing in the city night and mid-December's
    promised snow.

The neighborhood drunk yells
"Good night to be sober!"
I laugh, filling the silence, drunk on the stillness.

Manhattan blinks across the river
startled from her midnight trance
and I am big, like a man,

sleek like a leopard,
a wisp of wind,
a slice of moonlight, untouchable.

The children are asleep.
And I,
I am a silver fish,

the swish of a gray wolf's tail,
the lift of the falcon's wing,
a twist of light.

I am a piece of this winter's night
shadow on shadow
breath on breath.

I am.

Beacon, NY

2000–2001

Ritual creates its own catharsis. . . .
Metaphysical acts create mystical beliefs.

—Lauren Groff, *Matrix*

14

Gifts for a new home:
- *a libation of honey and whiskey for the land spirits*
- *an offering of salt and bread for the household gods*
- *a clean broom so you don't drag the schmutz from your past life into your fresh start*

"Put that one in the kitchen!" I hollered over my shoulder as I hefted my own box and headed up the stairs. The treads wore a dust-colored shag, but I'd already pulled up the tacks; there was oak underneath.

It felt miraculous that this house was mine. I'd owned it for two hours and thirty-seven minutes and already loved it with the kind of fierce joy usually reserved for puppies and red pandas. Even after sleeping on a sorry motel mattress in order to be up north to make the 8:30 a.m. closing, I was giddy with excitement as my Brooklyn friends arrived to help carry in boxes of kitchenware, Hefty bags of clothes, and furniture—a mattress, a chair that I'd found by the curb on trash day, the skinny pine table from the Chelsea Flea Market, and a pair of Adirondack chairs I'd purchased the week before from a friend's parents. Someone had hooked up the CD player and Sheryl Crow was "Leaving Las Vegas." Downstairs, Darlene sang along, unselfconscious and off-key. From the kitchen, I could hear Penny harmonizing. She had insisted on scrubbing the insides of the cabinets before putting anything away. When I dropped off the last box, she'd been kneeling on the counter, reaching yellow-gloved hands into each upper. I started moving the pile of "bedroom" boxes from the front hall to the actual bedrooms. At the top of the stairs, the vibrations of the stereo's bass thrummed under my feet, as if the house itself were humming along. My chest felt like it was cracking open. My house. *My house!* I had a house!

Hinges creaked as I pushed open the bedroom door with my shoulder. During the time I lived there, that door never did learn to stay open so, in true form, it swung mostly closed behind me. The box went into the closet, a cheap Sheetrock contraption added a century after the house was built. I stepped over the splotchy wine-colored stain on the oak floor, the one that sent icy skitters up my arms. There was something a little too bloody for comfort about that splotch. Resolutely, I stared it down. Blood or no, it was not going to keep me from taking the largest bedroom for myself.

My new home was in a small, industrial town an hour and a half's train ride north of Manhattan. It was a place I'd never visited prior to house hunting, in an area where I knew exactly one person—my Brooklyn roommate's mom.

Maybe it was a giant dose of desperation that sent me north. . . .

. . . Maybe magic was feeling mischievous and sprinkled pixie dust into my morning latte. . . .

. . . Or maybe the seed had been planted a few years back, the night I heard the katydid chorus during my grandma's shiva. Ever since that evening, I'd had a niggling sense that my soul wasn't singing along with the hum of cars on the Brooklyn-Queens Expressway, that something needed to shift. But, as with many seeds, there's a period of dormancy between an idea's inception and its germination. Dormancy isn't unusual in the plant world: Some seeds need a cold snap, while others need fire to melt their resinous core. This little seed, the one planted the night of the katydids, was awakened by, of all things, a trip to the Bronx.

Little-known fact: the borough now called the Bronx was, in the early days of the New Netherland colony, the farm of one Jonas Bronck and family. Three hundred fifty years later, when I rode the 6 train north from Manhattan, there was little left of that pastoral landscape except, perhaps, in the fairy-tale kingdom that was Taqwa Community Farm, a garden built from scraps, odd parts, and a whole lot of determination. I remember crossing the invisible threshold into the garden: my shoulders unhitched, and I smiled at George. We'd met through a volunteer group where I was helping with research and documentation of the city's community gardens as part of my master's thesis. Although it was well into October, late-season veggies stood tall in their straw-strewn beds. The crumbled remains of old masonry walls were covered in honeysuckle. "I haven't been here since Friday," George told me. "I come in, I'm touching everything. Walkin' around, touchin' everything. It's a good place to be. It's home."

Something in his words reminded me of the moments during my grandmother's shiva when I sat outside and spoke to the earth and it seemed to talk back. I didn't hear the voice of the earth in Brooklyn or Manhattan. Being there pulled me out of myself, sometimes so far out I felt disembodied, spun from wind and words and the electric current of ideas. Watching George doting on his kale and spinach made me nostalgic for something I couldn't quite name—something that twisted behind my sternum like the calligraphy of some long-forgotten language. Now I think of this sensation as my inner witch knocking on the door, letting me know there's an opportunity brewing and I should be paying attention. Then, I didn't grasp what the feeling was or how to answer it, so when I sensed the internal swooping and swirling, I'd either go for one of my rare evening runs or I'd ride the train. It was one of these train rides that took me north along the Hudson River to a village called Cold Spring. It quickly became a favorite place to visit.

One afternoon in July, having just returned from such an excursion, I had an email. It was from the school outreach director at the 92nd Street Y where I'd been taking poetry classes. The Y sponsored artist residencies at various New York City public schools. *Congratulations!* the email read. *I'm thrilled to inform you that we have accepted your proposal to create an elementary school poetry project for the 1999–2000 school year. Let me know when we can get together to discuss.* The stipend was also listed: for two days of work a week, I would be paid more than my full-time teaching salary at the Illustrious Private School. I had already decided to leave; relations with Claire were too strained. So this made the choice easy.

And if I only had to be in the city two days a week . . . maybe, just maybe, I could leave Brooklyn altogether.

My mind stretched back along the train tracks, following the gray-green depths of the Hudson, to a bench on the river and the sun setting behind the mountains. In a shadowy corner of my psyche, something new began to take shape.

15

Once you've found your house (you'll know by the inexplicable pull in your chest), begin to weave it into your story. Start by picturing yourself standing outside of it, on the sidewalk or in the garden. Admire its doors and windows, the jaunty set of its roof. The next day, imagine yourself walking up to the front door. Look out from there, seeing the views as the house does. On the third day, use your visualization to go inside.

Each day until the house is yours, send your spirit to explore its rooms and corridors. Be sure to shower the house with love. If you don't feel it back, this one might not be yours.

Sadly, I couldn't afford a thimble in Cold Spring. Beacon, not nearly so quaint, was the next town up.

My real estate agent met me at the station. I climbed into her Jeep, grateful the heater was cranked high to ward off the cold-damp of a February's morning. We turned off Main Street, heading into one of the older neighborhoods for our first appointment. The buildings were mixed: brick and industrial, then a little row of duplexes. Sprinkled in were working-class Victorians and a few Craftsman cottages. On the left we passed a pale blue house with a wraparound porch. Behind the chain-link fence, the lawn was spotted with late-winter slush. There was a tiny garage, too small for a modern car. *Ooo! An outbuilding.*

"I wish that one was for sale," I said aloud. It wasn't that the house was so very special or even well-kept. My interest came from something internal, as if my inner witch were tapping her nails against the sixties linoleum countertops the kitchen surely possessed. As I gazed at it, my brain began reworking the outbuilding into a garden shed with a deep soapstone sink and aged marble counters lined with seed starts. *I wish that one was for sale,* I thought again, looking back as we turned the corner.

"But it's not," my agent replied crisply, her tone imploring me to focus. Her green-gloved hand was holding a stack of printouts for the houses we were going to look at. "Any of these?" she asked, handing them to me. I pulled off my own gloves to thumb through the pile. *Ugh,* I thought, looking at homes I could only describe as drab and drabber. But what did I expect for $87,000?

———————

Three weeks later, my realtor called me midday. I was teaching poetry at an elementary school in Harlem on Tuesdays and Fridays so, on Wednesday, I was home to answer the phone.

"Remember that Victorian you liked?" she asked. "This is crazy, but it just came on the market! How soon can you get here?"

I knew, even before I'd hung up the phone, that it was mine.

When I say the house was both magic and Victorian, people's eyebrows go up, and their mouths form a little *O* before they say, *Like the* Practical Magic *house!?*

Let me assure you, my Beacon home had as much in common with the *Practical Magic* house as a Chihuahua has with a Weimaraner.

While the *Practical Magic* Victorian was a perfectly preserved confection of white clapboard and polished walnut, my new house came complete with water-stained drop ceilings, vinyl tile (held on by thick glue that came off with painstaking applications of boiling water and a scraper), and a metal front door that was significantly smaller than the doorframe; its vast width was filled in with multiple pieces of plywood. The outbuilding, it turns out, was a termite-eaten safety hazard. When my mother visited for the first time, she made it two steps inside before her eyes widened in horror...or terror. She reminded me of a horse I'd ridden as a teenager who would balk, roll his eyes, and shoot me aggrieved looks whenever I asked him to step through a puddle. As Mom opened her mouth to speak, my father, sensing impending doom, took her firmly by the elbow and guided her back to the sidewalk. They stood talking for a few minutes, their backs to the porch, before coming inside. Mom presented her best fake smile and said, "You have such vision!"

My first week in Beacon was a bustle. I scrubbed the kitchen with vinegar and lemon oil, grateful Penny had already taken care of the cabinets' innards. The bathrooms needed an application of something more industrial, so the windows were propped open for two days to diffuse the ammonia stink. Feeling cocky, I climbed up on a ladder and took down the drop ceiling, revealing the cracked plaster underneath. My realtor gave me a long vintage sofa, and I found a mostly comfy chair at a local antiques store.

It was the beginning of spring break, and everyone wanted to get out of the city. So I made regular trips to the train station, picking up friends whose platform boots and slinky sweaters looked comical in my seventies Formica kitchen (which, to my delight, was a whole decade newer than I'd projected when I first saw the house!). My ex-roommate arrived, bringing rosemary in a terra-cotta pot. Sitting on the front steps, we told stories and crushed the leaves until our fingers were sticky with memories. My ex-girlfriend showed up with JBL speakers she'd lugged all the way from Manhattan. We hooked them to my stereo, swapping out the hand-me-down set I'd gotten years before from my uncle—the ones she and I had used when we lived together. The speakers felt like the musical equivalent of a fresh broom.

Mrs. Cahill, my new across-the-street neighbor, brought a pie. The woman who owned the antiques shop came by with a bottle of wine. Two guys who lived down the block offered to help with the lawn until I got my own mower.

And then it dried up. It was as if I'd cashed in all my friendship chits. Through the remainder of the spring, I rode the train to Manhattan twice a week to teach poetry at P.S. 38 in Harlem. Even after teaching there for eight months, my days still felt disjointed and jarring. Some of the teachers had warmed to me after the Christmas holidays, when it became apparent that I was stubborn enough to stick out the year—it wasn't an easy assignment— but others remained distant; they knew I wasn't a long-hauler.

Back in Beacon, I learned how to caulk, paint, and peel wallpaper. I was extra careful with ladders and X-Acto knives: if I were to have an accident, no one would notice for weeks. In the evenings, I drank Merlot on the wrap-around porch and watched the sun set. The first month it was relaxing. The second month, it was simply lonely. In a fit of desperation, I found a barn and started teaching riding lessons. But, since my own horse had been sold while I was in college, riding had lost its luster.

By early August, the poetry residency was long over. My next steps, work-wise, were still amorphous. I was desperate for company, for something more exciting than, *After sending out ten resumes, I peeled five layers of wallpaper and it came down in one solid sheet, floor to ceiling! Yay, me!*

Then there was Simon.

Simon and I had been . . . what? Keeping each other company? Flirting relentlessly? Whatever it was, it had gone on for over a year. I wouldn't say he was my boyfriend. I'm not even sure he was a friend. Yet a month earlier, when I'd met him in Hearst Plaza for a picnic after teaching, he'd sat next to me on the curved concrete bench, his eyes lingering on the reflecting pool. "Never believe me if I say I don't love you," he'd murmured. I didn't know what to make of that. He was an enigma who sometimes showed up with sushi and a foot rub. His apartment was where I crashed when I stayed in the city too late. And there were benefits . . . just not *all* the benefits. To add to the confusion, I knew he'd been looking to escape Manhattan. And now he was coming to visit. I suddenly, desperately, wanted him to move in with me.

He arrived at the train station, tall, pale, and windblown. His hair always looked sideswept, like his curls grooved to the beat of an invisible industrial fan. He wasn't good-looking per se, but there was something shiny about him, something always darting from sunlight to shadow.

I'd planned the day like a seduction. From the train station, I skirted the edge of town, driving along the river, avoiding the more run-down parts of Beacon. Route 9D was lush, with the river on the right and a tumbled escarpment in shades of chartreuse on the left. Water trickled over boulders. A hawk circled, too high to identify. Alison Krauss sang from the CD player. I drove us south to Garrison, where we wandered country roads adorned with million-dollar mansions, then doubled back for lunch in Cold Spring. Simon had been jittery when he arrived, like he didn't know why he'd come. Maybe the scent of desperation was off-putting. But over lunch he began to relax, and by the time we'd secured lattes from the ice cream parlor, I was ready to drive him through Beacon.

Our tour started at the east end of town, the part that wasn't boarded over. I drove him past the antiques shop and the oh-so-SoHo hat and handbag boutique dreamed up by a pioneering Manhattan transplant. We cruised past the diner (*delicious omelets!* I chirped) and the auction house.

As we were about to turn onto my street, he asked, "Isn't the train station just ahead? I can catch the 2:20."

My heart stuttered. "Don't you want to see the house? You can catch the next train."

He looked like he was going to protest. He seemed content with the day as it was, with knowing he'd soon catch a train back to his Midtown apartment.

"Come on!" I said cheerfully. "It's just a few blocks down."

And I made the left turn.

This was the least complicated part of my seduction: I simply marched him up the stairs, tugging him into my bedroom and out of his clothing.

Without clothes he was long, almost silver, like a pike or a marlin leaping above the waves. Sunlight turned his skin golden to match his shoulder-length curls. His hands and feet were pale, stretched and lithe.

It all makes him sound like Adonis—which he wasn't. He was odd and sinuous and, in a way, almost bland. He didn't seem overly affected by the world and its opinions, so I didn't have to overthink him. He reminded me of the sea, which was somehow a comfort, and he smelled like nothing at all, which was a relief. In my mind, he was a creature of evenings, shade, and shadow. I hardly knew him in daylight.

Was I in love with him? I don't think so. His double-negative proclamation notwithstanding, it never seemed that he was in love with me either. He was an oddity and a convenience, but then, so was I. And while I wasn't in love with him, I was in love with the day we'd shared: with the way the light turned the leaves on Route 9 into a rainbow of translucent greens; with having someone make the ninety-minute trek from Manhattan for a visit; and even, truth be told, with the heft of my key ring as I opened first one lock, then the next, and brought him inside.

As I tugged Simon up the stairs, the tart taste of his reluctance coated my tongue. Perhaps I should have wondered why, in all those months we'd been together, we'd never had sex. And maybe it did drift across my mind, but I figured it was me: sex has never been a driving factor in my relationships.

Simon and I had met at a fundraiser for Kosovo, part of the project I had organized after my obnoxiousness at the Passover seder. The event took place at a trending venue; there were a few B-list celebs both entertaining and attending. It was a rush of adrenaline, cheek kisses, flirting, and phone numbers. I seemed, perhaps, to be someone I wasn't. It occurred to me now, staring at the rust-colored splotch that marred the bedroom's hardwood floor, that without the backdrop of Manhattan, maybe it had become apparent that I was never going to become the person he wished me to be.

But the joy of the day was bubbling through me: the happiness of multiple rooms instead of a studio apartment, the softness of sunshine as it slanted across the sheets. *I got to have all this.* It was miraculous. It was like my heart was singing *mine!* and I wanted, if only for a moment, for him to be mine too.

So we tumbled into bed, and he was long and lean and gentle. The world went fuzzy for a moment and my thoughts stilled as a spark—like a match struck in the darkness—lit up the shrouded spaces within me.

16

A jam of bilberry and black currant will help you see in the dark. Consume generously, preferably on toast with tea. Alternately soak three saffron threads in a half cup of red or white wine. Sip slowly.

There's a flash deep within the cosmos of a woman's womb at the moment when egg meets sperm, as if the body were sending up fireworks to mark the union. Scientists call this mini-pyrotechnic display a "Zinc Spark."

Our bodies register things our minds dismiss, which is why our bodies are a perfect doorway to connect us with the moon-drenched landscapes of intuition. We can see in the dark—if only we let ourselves.

17

In the brothels of Seattle, back before we had diaphragms and morning-after pills, wild carrot seeds were kept in a crystal dish in the parlor. The seeds were ground or taken as tea, the tour guides say. But beware! Wild carrot, also called Queen Anne's lace, looks much like poison hemlock, which will have less desirous effects.

I poured my fifth glass of milk.

Simon's dad came into the kitchen as I was returning the plastic jug to the fridge.

"The only time I've seen a woman drink that much milk was when she was with child," he said with a smile, leaning back against the worn butcher block countertop. Watery sunlight worked its way through the small window over the sink. "Do you want anything else? I think there might be cookies in the pantry," he added.

While my mind wants to add a layer of innuendo, my memory resists. Instead, my recollection is of a kind, slight man making simple conversation with his son's not-quite-girlfriend. He was probably just as baffled by my appearance in his home as I had been when Simon, whom I hadn't seen since he'd come to visit, suddenly phoned and proposed a trip to his parents' place in New Hampshire. It was September. I'd had a rough summer, contracting Lyme disease early on and having it misdiagnosed for all of July. It was mid-August before someone finally said *that mind-melting headache's not a sinus infection, that's Lyme disease!* By that point, I was losing words and my speech had begun to slur. When Simon reappeared and invited me to visit his family, the thought of letting someone else take care of me for a weekend was enough to make me cry. And staring out the car's window, watching the leaves turn to flame as we drove north through Massachusetts, had been a blissful meditation.

The milk was soothing. It was whole milk, which I never bought for myself. The thickness coated my teeth and throat; its coolness calmed me.

"No thanks on the cookies. This is perfect," I said, saluting Simon's dad with my half-empty glass.

I'd like to think I was smart enough to have had an "oh shit!" moment immediately, standing in the dimly lit kitchen with the refrigerator door halfway closed. When he first spoke, my back was to the room. I could have schooled my face back to neutral and let the fridge air cool my flush. But that wasn't what happened. Instead, I stood at the island, guzzled another glass of milk, and explained to the presumptive granddad that the antibiotics I'd been on for months made me nauseous and screwed with my taste buds.

Later, alone in the guest bedroom, replaying the day in my mind, I skipped right over the milk episode. Perhaps it was the archaic phrase "with child" that threw me off. Maybe it was the Lyme. Maybe it was simply more pleasant to ruminate on the salt-scented breeze and the sun warming my legs as Simon and I sat on a jetty near Portsmouth watching the fishing boats come in to unload their catches. I'd gorged on ice cream: two scoops of mint chip slathered with hot fudge. Simon had been almost chivalrous, chasing down my napkin before the wind could carry it out to sea.

My obtuseness firmly in place, I thought nothing of drinking Pepto-Bismol straight from the bottle the whole drive home.

18

Sometimes there is no answer that the waking mind can hold and handle. In these instances, take your hurts and confusions to your dreams. Write your pain on a scrap of paper. Put the paper into a pouch along with rose petals for healing, motherwort for dreaming, and black tourmaline for protection. Place this pouch under your pillow. For seven nights, set the intention to dream, allowing your subconscious to find resolution. When you feel complete, burn the scrap of paper.

My journal from the year 2000 is small and spiral-bound. The cover, softened by years, has a Japanese block-print feel, with green grasses and small starlike flowers. I'm picky about journals. There are multiple considerations: stitched or spiral-bound, hard- or softcover. The pages are always unlined, thick, and creamy.

The 2000 book was bought on one of my train excursions to Cold Spring, back when I still lived in Brooklyn. I remember a small shop, with the owner, slight and gray-haired, reading behind the checkout desk. A center table displayed a curated selection of novels and notebooks and, oddly, a rainbow of disposable fountain pens. I'd never seen a disposable fountain pen. I was entranced and went home with one in indigo, an inky rendition of the color Maxfield Parrish used for his twilit skies.

The journal was a small rectangle, appropriate for notes on the subway or at small round coffee shop tables. When I got home, it went on a shelf, waiting to be called into service. It seemed right to take it on my first train trip to Beacon, and after that the notebook slowly filled with mortgage details, notes on home renovations, and tales of my comical attempts to cohabitate with a pair of adopted Siamese cats.

In that small, thick notebook, the abortion was on the second-to-last page. There was little lead-up. It seemed to warrant only a note and the date.

After which there's nothing for four days.

Then:

Perhaps the moments of change fell between the pages, in the white space of days when I couldn't pick up a pen and wouldn't get out of bed. Or maybe they're buried here, between the house plans and poetry, and someday I'll reread this little book and understand how I got to the place where my only certainty is uncertainty and that pure white joy I'd been circling 'round has become shrouded in fog-gray. . . . It feels right that this book is ending; I've changed; it's time to start again.

And then nothing again until a new book begins January 1, 2001.

———————

When I try to remember the weeks before the abortion, I catch glimpses of a room, sterile, no windows. The nurse is looking at an ultrasound screen. She turns to tell me something, but then glances at my chart. Still, in my mind, she says: *It's a boy!* I now know it would have been too early for her to make such a determination, but I didn't know that then. So the scene remains as I first envisioned it.

The weekend before the procedure, I drove to Baltimore, to my friend Tracy, who was a nurse midwife. I wanted to try herbs before going the surgical route and didn't want to be alone if it worked. It didn't: I was too far along for pessaries and tinctures.

More than the pain of the abortion, it is this failure—the inability to end the pregnancy myself—that haunts the pages of my journal:

I was so sure I could squat in the woods and give the baby back to the earth, soul to the sky, not a metal tube sucking.

79

Perhaps this was magical thinking. It's still difficult for me to distinguish between the everyday magic inherent in the world and the magic found only in books. Books were where I had first discovered magic, and stories, after all, always hold a grain of truth. How big is that grain? Are magical tales mostly make-believe or are there people, right now, levitating and moving objects with their minds?

Recently, I asked some witchy friends if they knew anyone who could light a candle without a match. I half thought a friend would look at me like I was nuts, snap her fingers, and light every candle in her home.

Am I the only one who can't send smoke coiling through the tinder simply by pointing a finger?

"Ha, ha!" one friend laughed at my question, then "Wait, are you serious?"

This isn't a new preoccupation. One night, still in the blue Beacon Victorian, I spent a half hour staring at a candle's wick, rhythmically chanting *light, light, light*. When that didn't work, I attempted to find the flame in my heart, pushing the feeling of fiery love toward the wick. Nothing. Then there was a final attempt: I would *be* the flame and then merge my energy with the candle's. The candle, suddenly knowing its true purpose, would spontaneously ignite. I focused on everything within me that had fiery energy.

One at a time, I called up the passions of love, of rage, of righteousness. I honed in on those red-hot sensations, the way they felt in my gut and jaw, and visualized bundling them into a ball of pure flame. Then, because even mid-visualization I was worried about burning down the house, I compressed the fire so I could, with laser precision, touch it to the wick. My eyes were closed. I was radiating heat and orangey light. *Was that a trickle of smoke I smelled?* I smiled. *I'd figured it out! I'd found the secret!*

As I prepared to open my eyes, I first actively imagined flickers against my lids to reinforce the concept of light. A deep breath, then OPEN!

The dining room came into focus. I was sitting on the oak floor. A tapered cream candle sat in an iron holder in front of me. The white cotton wick rose like an antenna, unscorched and not even a smidge warm.

This inability to call fire haunts me still. I feel certain that if I could have lit a candle, I could also have willed my womb to empty itself. Were there women who could squat in the woods on the night of a waning moon and sing the cells that wanted to multiply back to the earth? It's the mechanism of the abortion that offends me, not the fact of it. There is something sacred in knowing your own rhythms, understanding which seasons are for creation and which for letting go, and in allowing the necessary dieback that will, after a fallow time, produce healthier life.

Go from whence you came—back to my cells, my bones, my blood. Now is not the time to be separate from me. Live within me. See this world through my eyes, feel this world through my hands. This is the life I can give you. This is the choice I have made for us both.

I wonder what I thought about during those journal-less days. If I ever put my hand on my belly, contemplating the way generations nest one inside the next. If I had felt the hand of Atropos, eldest of the Fates, lightly touching my shoulder when I decided to snip the thread, to say *this line of lineage ends with me.*

In 2001's journal—a tall notebook decorated with swirling blue cranes—I found clues to what my life looked like during the unrecorded months at the end of 2000: a friend of a friend, Quinn, moved into one of the guest rooms while she was temporarily broken up with her boyfriend. Luckily, she continued to live with me even once they got back together. Quinn laughed at everything. She was whip-smart and thoughtful but rarely serious. I think it sometimes drove her boyfriend batty, but her boisterous energy was an excellent buffer when Simon moved in. (Yes, that happened.)

His stay was short and strained. His face always looked starched, stern; I remember that now. It seems I vacillated—*I love him; I love him not.* When my step-grandpa, who had none of my blood, but all of my heart, died in Decem-

81

ber of 2000, my journal tells me that Simon had hardly a kind word. Hardly a word at all. . . .

I love him not.

He soon left to take a job in Boston.

The 2000 notebook remains blank on the death of my grandpa. How did I mourn him? What words did I say as his body was lowered into the earth? I don't even remember his funeral.

Flipping forward through the months of 2001, I reach the pages for early May. I had begun to see an acupuncturist named Gail for a searing pain in my abdomen—my body reacting to an ovarian cyst too small to be medically significant. Gail brought to mind a hobbit, her home office tiny and set in the old growth of the forest, like a burrow in the woods. It took two gravel roads to get to her.

When we first met—after I was referred by my physician—I had no idea how foundational she would be to the person I was becoming. Over a few years of seeing her, going to her home through many seasons and at various hours of the day, I often had the sensation of entering some sort of liminal space as I crossed the threshold. I would park Rosie under a sunlit elm, but somehow twilight would set in by the time I had crossed the yard, traversed the steps, and cruised through the front door, which was always held wide in welcome.

That first day, after the paint-crusted screen slammed behind me, we sat at the walnut dining table to go over my intake form. Midway through our chat, Gail got up and came back with a wall calendar. Her curly dark head tilted as she flipped backward through the pages. Photos of spring tulips gave way to winter's snow. Autumn leaves changed to wheat fields, harvest ready and blowing in the wind. Counting back through the months, we worked out the timeline and realized that the pain had started about nine months from when Simon had come to visit. Nine months from conception. The pain had begun near what would have been my due date.

My mind never struggled with the decision to have an abortion. There was nothing stable in my life. I'd been on antibiotics for Lyme disease for months. My house was most likely riddled with lead paint and lead pipes, and it was definitely full of carpet tacks—so many carpet tacks. Plus, I believed the planet was overpopulated: I didn't want to contribute to the next generation. But mostly, I had known, with one-hundred-percent certainty, that motherhood wasn't my path.

Still, although my mind had been settled, my body obviously was not. A two-centimeter, medically insignificant cyst shouldn't have caused the kind of pain I had been feeling. Trying to remember if there was some other mitigating factor, I paged through my journal.

And there it was, noted not immediately after the abortion but in the recounting of it to Gail. The doctor had performed the abortion without local anesthesia or painkillers—because, he said, "Drugs make women too emotional."

I hadn't remembered this particular piece of misogyny. How the doctor had sculpted my experience, turning what could have been sacred into an exercise in endurance and pain. Into a trauma that lingered in my cells for months.

19

Many times upon a time, there was a witch.

The witch lived in a house with a wild garden. . . .

The witch lived near the fields where she could gather herbs. . . .

The witch lived in the city but knew the lore of leaf and root.

Raspberry leaves to prepare the womb,

Lady's Mantle to call the sacred,

Nettles to nourish new life,

Black Cohosh to welcome it forth.

Shepherd's Purse to staunch the bleeding,

Fennel to bring down the milk,

Sage to dry it up.

I can't think about the abortion without my mind tumbling through the centuries, visiting the anonymous healers, midwives, and abortionists who have been called *witch*. These women navigated the space between life and death. We often forget, now, how many women died in childbirth, how many babies failed to make it through the canal. With pills and patches, many no longer need those who dug roots and made potions to keep the womb an empty vessel.

But I feel them sometimes, lingering by the raspberry patch or ghosting up from my own depths, reminding me of the fine line between this world and the next.

20

To heal from birthing, make a bath tea with equal parts dried comfrey leaf, calendula flowers, lavender flowers, yarrow flowers, and witch hazel blossoms. Steep, covered, for thirty minutes. Strain well. Add to bathwater. Repeat daily.

It was May, and I was planning a baby shower. The invitations were sent, the refreshments planned, and now Quinn and I were at the garden center searching for just the right tree.

Gail had suggested I find a way to ritualize giving birth. It sounded goofy, but I was willing to give it a try. Anything to appease my furious womb and ovaries. So my friends were coming for a baby shower. I planned to give birth to a healthy baby bush.

As I walked up and down the gravel paths lined with burlap-balled bushes, my fingers trailed over the leaves of wild roses and the early blooms of forsythia. A viburnum? A lilac? The choices were nearly overwhelming.

The bees thought so too, darting from plant to plant, searching out the early bloomers. Down a side aisle were the less showy varieties. It was there I found a little shrub with strange, and nearly spent, spindly flowers hanging from the branches like yellow daddy longlegs. I stood in front of it feeling a sense of . . . communion? Maybe. Maybe that one. I moved down the aisle, dreaming of wisteria (no, it could grow huge and damage the house) or magnolia (it would be miserable, or dead, after a Beacon winter, Quinn assured me, her laugh quirky and barking).

The path wound around to the board-and-batten garden shop, its porch bedecked with wind chimes and suncatchers. I felt kind of floaty as I wandered up the steps—as if I were invisible. Quinn had gone off to check out perennials for one of her gardening clients. From the porch, I watched her compact form recede, her supernova energy moving away from me like a pulsing light on a radar screen. I was unmoored. No one knew me here in this cozy space stacked with flowerpots and bedazzled with hummingbird feeders. I was anyone. I was no one. My fingers ran over the glaze on the pots. None were as detailed as the one I'd brought with me from Jan's house, currently in the front bay window where the spotted begonia could sun itself.

Tomorrow, in true baby-shower style, everyone was bringing gifts for the baby bush. I hadn't decided what I would give it beyond a place in the yard. Chimes sounded gently as someone came through the door. I'd taken the wind chimes from Jan's garden before I moved out. They were tucked in a corner of the porch, waiting to be hung from the rafters. *Hmm.* . . . In a corner, there were metal shepherd's crooks, the kind you spike into the ground. I could hang the chimes by the sapling. . . .

The sapling I still needed to choose.

Leaving the crook by the register, I headed back out, rewalking my path. This time, when I got to the daddy-longlegged plant, I was certain. Before picking up the black plastic pot, I read the tag: *witch hazel*—a plant I later learned was used to stop bleeding after an abortion or miscarriage.

We gathered in the morning. Quinn had already dug the hole. The women came in sun hats and braids for the party, with boots on for the planting. Friends from Beacon, Brooklyn, and Baltimore introduced themselves, awkwardly choosing hugs over handshakes. Which started the laughter. And the shoulder bumping. And the sense of something building in the air around us.

I carried the little tree, which we had named Hazelton, and set it next to the hole. A breeze skipped through, rustling hair and hats. Takeout cups and travel mugs were nestled into the grass as people sat, curled, or stretched onto the earth. Then everyone quieted as Quinn and I shimmied Hazelton out of his pot and carefully lowered him into the ground. I picked up the shovel, backfilling the dirt, struck by how similar it felt to throwing dirt into the open hole that had held my grandmother's coffin. In my heart, I said goodbye to the parts of me that had been extracted and, hopefully, in some way returned to the earth. If not at the time, at least symbolically now. And then, even though I was still angry with him, I opened my heart to Simon and the part of *him* that had been returned to the earth, to the "us" that had been aborted. I apologized to my body, to my being, for the promises printed in the secret language of pheromones—ones I'd been unable to keep.

Quinn took the shovel, ready to make quick work of the hole, her buff arms flexing as she scooped. But a friend from work got to her feet. Drifting up behind Quinn, she said, "Let me." Beth, who ran the local antiques shop, stood up next and took the shovel. With unplanned solemnity, each woman added a small amount of dirt and then gave me a hug before finding a place in the circle we'd inadvertently created. The last person smoothed the dirt with her hands, settling it like a baby. Quinn had unrolled the hose and pulled it closer. Everyone was silent as she gave the witch hazel its first drink.

We sat for many moments, heads tipped up to the sun or down to the earth. A crow cawed, then a robin trilled. Someone hiccoughed. We giggled. The moment unfroze. Gifts were pulled out: sweets, which we passed around; a Tupperware container of chicken poop, for Hazelton (we laughed uproariously); *The Giving Tree* by Shel Silverstein (we read it, cover to cover, sitting round the circle); and finally, a small suncatcher, amazingly shaped like a butterfly. It hung from the branches, catching the light. Quinn helped me spike the shepherd's crook into the ground and Jan's wind chimes sighed. I took a deep breath and let my ghosts go—the one in my head, the one in my blood, the one in my heart, and the one in my womb.

Despite the pain, the abortion and what followed are a rite of passage I would traverse again. It began a series of lessons that ultimately taught me that I am not a disembodied mind trapped in a suit of flesh, but instead an integrated being whose senses and intelligence extend far beyond the confines of my brain. Untangling the spiral of my body's pain was the first step. Actually, that's not quite right. Realizing my body could hold pain and trauma without my mind's awareness was the first strand of the web. Everything else spooled from that understanding.

If every bit of me had intelligence, and not just my brain, what else did I know without my mind realizing it?

The answers that came from this line of questioning opened a path to integration not only within my physical being, but within the larger world. Because my body (and yours) connects with the cycles of the moon and the turning of the seasons, it houses senses beyond the well-known five and rhythms for which we hardly have words. Knowing this, feeling this, allowed me to align with the world in a way I never had before. If my body knows the moon, then I am in a relationship with the moon. If my internal clock ticks with the changing seasons, then I am like the magnolia and the marmot who also shift with the seasons.

There are many pathways to this knowing. For me, these lessons came in the wake of the abortion. This is how I found my way to the thing I can comfortably call magic. The books in my high school backpack, the pulsing light after Jan died, the birthday ritual of tarot card spreads, the slow and steady departure I was making from a reliance on Western medicine—these were all clues, but I needed the sensations in my body, the knowings that came as I moved through the months post-abortion, to begin to accept these changes.

I still can't light a candle with a thought. Instead, my magic is of gentle knowings and cyclical living, of letting my body sink into the rhythms of the cosmos and quietly using those rhythms to spin and reweave the web of my own future.

21

The earliest acupuncture needles were sharpened bone and bamboo and stone. Animal, vegetable, mineral, connecting us back to both ourselves and the earth. What webs would you lay upon your body to weave yourself home?

"How's the pain since the tree planting?" Gail asked.

At first it was odd to lie on the acupuncture table, naked under a sheet, and chat. *Maybe this is what psychoanalysis feels like,* I thought, with the therapist out of your sightline so that you feel as if you're talking mostly to yourself.

"So much better! It's weird, right?" I was still trying to wrap my head around how planting a tree could resolve ovarian pain, how a ritual could satisfy the howling of my uterus. It mostly made no sense . . . but somehow it sort of did.

Gail started putting in needles. Bright points of pain flashed as they connected with the other needles, a spiderweb laid over my body. My face twitched.

"The body has its own knowledge, its own truths," Gail said. "It has a lot to teach us, if we let it."

She put in one final needle at the crown of my head. The web of pinpricks lit up, then subsided. I winced.

Patting my foot, she said, "Rest now. Focus on your breath." She turned down the lights as she left, closing the door behind her.

I floated in the darkness, seeing in my mind the web of needles, their pattern etched in fiery lines on my eyelids. My face spasmed, and my nose twitched. I saw a panther. I was a panther. My nose scrunched again. I was a wolf. I turned my amber gaze on myself, watched myself float. I breathed. I twitched. I floated.

The lights came up slowly. I was woozy. Gail's face swam over mine.

"Hold on," she said, leaving the room.

A minute or an hour later—I could never say for sure—she returned. "Open your mouth," she instructed. Onto my tongue she popped a square of chocolate, bitter and dark. "This will help you get back in your body," she said, smiling over me. I sucked the chocolate as she shifted around the table, removing the needles, unweaving the web.

"Okay! Take your time. Come out when you're ready."

My limbs felt heavy, but my heart felt light. What had just happened? I was somehow more me than when I had arrived. I fumbled with the zipper on my jeans, trying to remember how fingers worked. I saw feathers, flashed on paws. Straightening my shirt, I looked in the mirror, grounding myself in the familiar contours of my own face, staring into my eyes.

When I emerged from the treatment room, Gail was sitting at her dining room table making notes in my chart. The house felt once more like a hobbit burrow, especially this room, with its dark walnuts and sage greens. The hobbit looked up from her writing. "Great job!" she said. "You're all done. I don't need to see you again."

What?

That was not what I wanted to hear. I mean, sure, I wanted the cyst healed, but there was something else here, something in this space, or in Gail, or in the needles. And it was something I needed. I'd found a path to a nameless place I'd been searching for. My inner witch rustled in the depths of my psyche. I remembered the Hero's Journey.

Gatekeeper, my subconscious supplied, the word floating up through layers of self.

"I think, maybe, I still need to see you," I said tentatively.

Gail raised an eyebrow. "You go home and think about that," she said briskly. "Because if you come back, it's going to get a lot harder."

I went back.

It became harder.

It became easier.

I'd learned enough by then to know that when I accepted a call to adventure instead of fighting it, events unfolded with a little more ease.

And, it turned out, after I said "yes" and stepped through the portal, I was surrounded by mentors.

I'd arranged a lecture with herbalist Barbara Hall for students at SUNY Purchase, where I'd gotten a job in the Student Activities office. In a dingy, windowless room in the basement of the Student Activities Building—as far from magical and mystical as you could possibly get—Barbara stood in front of a painted cinder block wall looking a little peaked under the fluorescent lights. She was explaining how to pick an herbal remedy for yourself.

"Stand with your feet square on the ground, and pass the herb through your chakras," she instructed.

She'd flipped her long hair—wheat streaked with gray—over her shoulder before beginning, as if the gesture would leave her chakras in clear view.

"When you get to your root chakra . . . ," she said, hovering the jar she was holding in front of her pubic bone, "hold it there and see whether you move toward or away from it."

My stomach gave a little flip. *No friggin' way,* I thought, mortified. This lecture had been my idea; I was never going to live this down. Up until now, the talk had been the basics of herbalism: use this for that—nettle for nutrients, raspberry leaf to tone the uterus. Basically what I had learned reading *Prescriptions*. Barbara had also gone over how to harvest: away from the road and any place that might be sprayed with pesticides; and be careful with your plant ID! These things were . . . *real*. Even if most doctors didn't think about it, herbs had chemical constituents just like pharmaceuticals, so of course, they could shift the chemistry of the human body. And the harvesting information was just plain common sense. But this pass-it-through-your-chakras stuff? This was whack-a-doodle. Even with what I was learning about the intrinsic wisdom of the body, this was asking for a bit too much faith. It was certainly not university-level fodder. Barbara had passed a mason jar of herbs to the first volunteer. As awe-filled students jumped up to give it a try, I watched, fluctuating between embarrassed and mortified.

And it was about to get worse.

"Come on up and give it a go, Em!" Barbara trilled.

I looked at the rapt faces around me and wanted to bury my head in my hands. Instead, I stifled my sarcastic smirk and joined Barbara at the front of the room. She passed me a mason jar filled with dried motherwort, repeating, "Just pass it in front of your chakras."

I planted my feet on the floor, hip distance apart, raised the jar to the height of my third eye, and began slowly moving it downward, holding the jar about a foot from my body. When I hit my solar plexus, I started to tilt forward. When the jar passed my navel, I lurched toward it, filled with shock as I tried to keep my balance.

"I think that was a *yes*," Barbara said dryly. "One cup of tea, three times a day."

––––––––––

That night, in my Formica-fronted kitchen, I filled and labeled five identical mason jars with tea, rat poison, cocoa powder, dishwasher granules, and granola. I closed my eyes as Quinn handed me one jar at a time, in no particular order. Passing each jar in front of my chakras just like Barbara had taught, I was flabbergasted to find that my body seemed to be able to read the energy of the item in the jar. Repeatedly. I leaned in toward the foods and pushed back from the poisons.

"No way!" Quinn laughed, her whole face smiling. Quinn's laugh was big and bright, sapping away my overly serious energy and lightening the air in the room. "I wanna try!"

So we set up the whole experiment again, letting Quinn's body be the pendulum. Her eyes popped open as she swayed toward the granola. We stared at each other for a beat, grinning maniacally. Her stomach growled.

"I wonder if it would work if you weren't hungry," I quipped, humor normalizing the awe zinging through my heart.

How was this possible?

On the face of it, it was absurd. I tried to remember other times I'd known something in a way I didn't understand.

An image flashed through my mind of standing in another kitchen, this time at the house where I'd grown up. In my memory, the phone is cradled between my cheek and shoulder, the mustard-colored cord wrapped around my legs. I dial my mom's number and announce, "I just got into U of M!" While I would soon learn this to be true, at the moment I made the call I hadn't yet walked down to the mailbox. I'd instead seen the postal worker pull up and put a handful of letters into the box. Watching him, I'd known with one-hundred-percent certainty that he had delivered a letter which would say I was accepted.

But that was a sparkly one-off moment. Sorting through my memories, I looked for another. There was the game I played my first day at architecture school, in which I looked around each classroom I entered, noting who I was drawn to most instinctually. Then I purposefully didn't sit with any of those people. Instead, I tried to make other friends, cultivating the folks who hadn't initially caught my eye. But by the end of the semester, I'd become friends with exactly those to whom I'd been instantly, and inexplicably, drawn. And then there was the dream the night my girlfriend's cat had died. In it, her mom cradled the cat like a baby, a halo over her head. When

I awoke, I knew the cat was gone. And I supposed I should also include the first time I saw the blue house, the house I was standing in, and thought *that one's mine.*

But that was it. If there were other instances of my intuition taking center stage, I couldn't think of them. But maybe that was the problem—the *thinking.* This sensing with my body felt different, more real somehow.

Lying on Gail's table later that week, I recounted the whole experience, from Barbara's lecture to Quinn's laugh.

"Told you. You know all sorts of stuff," Gail said, sliding in a needle. "Your body's constantly gathering information." She inserted another needle, a bright spark of pain webbed through the pattern she was drawing on my skin. "Start working with it consciously this week. We often mistake intuition for emotion. So pay attention to your emotions. See if you can find where each one lodges in your body."

Questions began to form in my mind: *What's the difference between a feeling and a thought? How does an intuition get confused with an emotion?* I tried to sift through them, to get concise, knowing Gail wasn't given to long explanations. But by the time I had my thoughts in order, she had dimmed the lights and left the room.

22

Poppy for dreamless sleep.
Ziziphus to soothe nightmares.
Mugwort to remember the dreamer's tales.

The Strawberry Moon chivvied through the open window, whispering in on a late-June breeze. It found me sleeping, although I felt wide awake.

The flagstones were cold and my feet calloused as I padded to the portico. The knock had been quiet, as if the knocker were afraid to disturb the night, but I'd been waiting. On the other side of the door there was a line of people. They held satchels and cloth bundles and wore layers of clothing, more than they needed for even a night as cool as this one.

I felt a sad smile crease my face as I pulled the door wider, letting them in. Once the last woman stepped through, swathed in three shawls and two skirts, I locked the door, pulling a wide oak bar into place.

The villagers waited patiently as I shifted a wardrobe on its hinges, opening a cavity in the stone wall. Stairs led into the darkness, and they began to slip down, one by one. When the last one was gone, I shifted the wardrobe back into place.

My sheets were smooth and the bed warm. A sense of surety, of knowing something I didn't know before, sat heavy on my chest. There are many types of dreams, I've learned. This type, where the storyline is solid and every sense engaged, is the rarest. I lay awake a long time remembering the feel of the flagstones on my feet and the robe chafing the tender skin along my ribs.

When I told Gail about the dream, she said, "Let's try something."

She put in a series of needles, lowered the lights, and left the room.

I swam in the in-between, my attention focusing on my throat. And then I was deep in memory, everything real and present.

My skin is hot. Smells—perfume, sweat, the faint scent of copal— overwhelming.

Listening to our tour guide, who is inches shorter than I am but somehow seems larger and more vibrant, I feel a spiraling in my spine, and I sway with it, a gentle metronome, back and forth, back and forth. Other tourists shuffle past like images on aging celluloid: windbreakers, khaki shorts, long black hair, a rhinestone purse, an odd-shaped skirt, the flash of an earring, a worn leather sandal. . . .

We climb to the top of one of the temples. I'm disoriented. I no longer try to focus on the guide's patter but hang back, waiting for the tour to end. Then a hand appears in my peripheral vision. The fingers close on my upper arm yanking me toward a worn limestone slab in the temple's center. In a controlled dip like a dance move, the tour guide lays me on the stone and, using the side of his hand, mimes cutting my throat. In my mind, I lay there, stunned, but in reality, he's already reaching out the hand that "cut" me, hauling me up, and patting me on the back as he thanks me for being a good sport. In the world of wind-breakers and khakis, it feels like we should take a bow.

Gail is standing at my shoulder when I surface, ready with a square of chocolate. She gives me a few moments, letting the chocolate melt on my tongue.

"Where did you go?" she eventually asks.

"Chichen Itza," I tell her, still seeing it behind my eyelids. "It was a family trip. I was sixteen. We climbed to the top of the temple. I was the"—I made air quotes—"sacrifice."

"Umm," she murmured noncommittally before asking, "Just that once?"

I was baffled, but she'd already closed the door. It took me a few days to work out what she'd been asking: Do I think our bodies only remember what has happened in this lifetime? Are dreams that feel like reality past life experiences? Do I believe in reincarnation?

I still don't know. Energy transmutes; it doesn't just disappear—sure. But does your entire consciousness or soul get transferred, intact, to another human body? I can't say for certain.

But there are things I have never learned in this body, in this timeline, that feel clear and real to me. So I try not to think about it too much. If I don't become attached to grand theories, I can just know what I know and feel what I feel.

23

When you ask the universe for a sign, allow the response to be subtle.
Let it be enough to be reminded that you are woven into the fabric of
life, that you are right where you're supposed to be.

After discovering I could use my body as a pendulum, I thought, *Maybe magic is real!*

Conversely, I also grew more skeptical. After seeking for so long, I didn't want to be duped; I didn't want to fool myself.

So I began asking the universe for signs: *show me that I'm on the right path; affirm that this is the best decision.*

When I asked, something small would often happen—I'd find a feather on my way into work, or the name of a person I'd been considering reconnecting with would also be the name of a new character on a favorite TV show.

But when I received these small signs, they'd seem too much like serendipity. Just to be certain, I'd ask for another, to prove to myself that the initial sign really, truly, was a sign.

In this way, I kept escalating the stakes, testing the universe. And so, as I learned to harness my intuition and step into my own magic, I found myself swimming in much deeper waters than was strictly necessary.

24

There is no spell that can soothe this day.

The sky was cerulean: crystalline and perfect. A quintessential autumn day.

Everyone I speak with who was in New York on 9/11 begins their recollection the same way: *the sky was so blue, the day so perfect.*

We've been trained by movies and television to expect cloud cover and an ominous soundtrack to foreshadow doom. But the morning of September 11, 2001, was filled with laughter and a sense of hope.

Though it was early, I'd already taken my new class outside and passed out "explorer" worksheets and tiny plastic magnifying glasses. While working at SUNY Purchase had interesting moments, the bright spots had glimmered amidst long stretches of boring. Used to the constant activity of a classroom, I chafed at the in-between times. While my colleagues took official-looking legal pads to the cafeteria where they chatted with friends, drank coffee, and pretended they were working, I paced my office, annoyed that I had to stay until five when my work was already done. Still, the spaciousness did leave plenty of time to secure a position at a small, experimental farm school for the 2001–2002 school year. The animals were supposed to teach responsibility and apparently kids like veggies better if they grow them themselves.

We were on the hillside next to the goats' paddock when five fighter jets flew overhead in tight formation. Thomas tugged on my sleeve to earnestly explain, "Em, those are fighter jets. They're from Steward Air Force Base. This is not their normal training route."

Up until that moment, I'd been so elated, so full of joy and hope for this new school year, so grateful for my students sitting on the school's hillside in pairs, working on their science lesson.

Angela crossed the driveway, her linen palazzo pants rippling in the breeze. She was in the administration but, I was told, occasionally taught drama. Slipping up beside me, she linked her elbow with mine and pushed her sunglasses up so they held her long curls off her face. I barely knew— but instinctively liked—her. She had a warm and open air and seemed less inclined to cliquishness than some of the other administrators. I was pleased she'd chosen to come out and say "hi" to me, the only new teacher on staff. She tugged me up the hill a little, the mowed grass soft under my bare feet.

"I need you to smile," she murmured. I must have started to say something or maybe I just looked confused. She squeezed my arm, staring into my eyes, and smiled a little brighter as if in demonstration. I mimicked her, pasting a fake smile on my face.

"Good," she murmured. She laughed, and I could hardly tell it wasn't real. I guess that's why she taught drama.

"Okay. I'm about to tell you something. I need you to hold it together. I'm going to tell you everything I know, so don't ask me any questions because this is all I've got."

And then she proceeded to explain to me that a plane had hit the North Tower of the World Trade Center. It took my brain a few seconds to understand. What a horrible accident! How was it even possible?

My mouth must have been opened because Angela squeezed my arm. "Smile," she reminded me.

The day had barely begun, but it had been decided that school was closing. Parents would be picking up their kids, but they could not be allowed into the building; that would be chaos. I was to bring my students inside and keep them in the classroom. Angela would come for them one at a time as their parents arrived. I was confused. Why were we closing? Sure, we had a few parents who worked downtown, but this seemed like an extreme reaction.

Angela saw my confusion. She swiveled to face me, turning me by the elbows so my back was toward the kids.

"Em, it wasn't an accident."

It wasn't an accident? It wasn't.... I tried to master my face. Behind me, the kids were shouting out their finds, combing the earth with their big magnifying glasses. I looked toward the sky, azure and flawless. Angela squeezed my arm.

"Other planes seem to have been hijacked. Parents want their kids home." She squeezed my elbows one last time and headed up the hill as five fighter jets streaked by again, thin and fast and loud.

Thomas tugged on my sleeve once more, pointing up, his voice a staccato of facts, "Steward Air Force Base, fighter jets, not their normal route." This time he sounded distressed.

"Wow!" I said brightly. "You know so much more about fighter jets than I do! How about you help me round everyone up, and then you can tell me about them on the way in?"

By ten o'clock the school was empty. *Get home,* we were told. *The Pentagon's been hit. A hijacked plane crashed in Pennsylvania. We don't know what's going on. Be safe.* Hugs were exchanged before we climbed into our separate cars and set out, each alone on the country roads, trying to find some news that made sense.

The farm school lost one parent. I learned later that the Illustrious Private School had, miraculously, lost none.

Tower Two, where I'd gotten coffee and made photocopies, had collapsed at 9:59 a.m. I'd been gathering lesson plans and books into my bag. The sky had been so very blue. I tried to remember the faces of the men—so many young men—who couldn't remember my name. I tried to remember what floor my college housemate had worked on, the name of her company.

The roads home were eerily empty. I stayed off the highway. I remember the viridian green of late summer, the cerulean blue of the sky, a voice on the radio, the words: *planes, bombs, terrorists, attack, dead.* The sound of the impact as the plane hit the North Tower played over and over, like a bomb detonating. There wasn't another car on the road. I passed a weatherworn white farmhouse I'd always liked, its welcoming front porch now sporting an oversize flag, red, white, and blue, blue, blue.

At home, Tracy, the midwife from Baltimore, was huddled on the couch. She sprang up when I walked in.

"Can you believe this?" she asked.

She'd been visiting to help me with renovations and had planned to leave that morning after rush-hour traffic. We'd said goodbye before I left for school. But the Hudson River bridges had been closed after the first plane hit, so she had stayed.

We sat in front of the television, clicking from station to station, trying to sort out what was going on. We watched people falling and jumping from the Towers over and over until Quinn came home and turned off the TV. We tried, again and again, to call Annette, our third housemate who had moved in over the summer. She was a Manhattan friend from the dinner club; we'd bonded over the cutting board as she demonstrated the proper way to devein shrimp to me, the only non-chef in the group. She was elegant—Sophia Loren in an apron—her long finger moving seamlessly to remove guts and tails.

Annette still worked in Midtown. She had left on the train that morning. We couldn't get through on the phone.

I took it all in. I was just learning the ways of the body and had no sense of self-preservation. I opened myself to the confusion, despair, pain, anger, and heartache. I traced their routes, found their locations under my skin—*I feel the grief here, the rage there, the pain everywhere.*

25

To ground yourself, rub sage oil on the soles of your feet (replace with lavender if you have epilepsy or seizures). Stand barefoot. Stretch your arms overhead, reaching through the rib cage. Imagine your feet becoming roots, spreading out, anchoring in. Your arms become branches, swaying, gently feeling the breezes of the world around you.

Grief closed my throat. Fear clenched my stomach. Rage had an upward trajectory, like liftoff, like puking.

In the weeks after 9/11, the farm school had asked us to have our classes say the Pledge of Allegiance. I couldn't do it. The request sat like liquid-lead deep in my gut. It reminded me of synagogue, of being handed a book of words and being told to say them.

This is how you pray. This is how you show patriotism.

Instead, I called the class to the rug and told them to bring notebooks. "Let's find our own words," I suggested.

It started off well enough. I prompted, "What does it mean to be patriotic, to love your country?" The answers were sweet and sometimes surprising: "It means being nice to each other." "It means we can say what we think. You can't do that in every country." "It means you should visit the capitals of all fifty states!" And then Tess: "It means other people don't like you because you have things they don't." I could hear her mom in that comment. "Sometimes they hate you a lot," Tess continued, sniffing. Her eyes filled up. And then her head was in her hands and she was sobbing. Julia moved closer, so they were shoulder to shoulder. And then *she* sniffed. I got up and grabbed a box of tissues off my desk.

I don't know what happened in the seven seconds my back was to them, but when I turned, the neat circle was clumped like old blood. The silks anchoring the group had slipped free; the web was curled in upon itself.

Time stopped. I was at a loss. It seemed the wind was blowing. I could feel the box of tissues held loose in my hand, my long skirt swirling round my ankles.

Thomas moved toward the plastic bin of Legos. A tower went up quickly. He smacked it with his palm, and it went flying as he puffed his cheeks and said *pooouufff!*

I unfroze. I handed Amelia the tissues and went to crouch by Thomas.

"What's this?" I asked.

"Like on TV," he said, focused on reconstructing the tower.

He was watching this on TV? He was nine years old!

Tower completed, a little Lego man was perched on the top, his square base connecting him to the tower's top. Then Thomas reached out a finger and flicked. The Lego man went flying. Oh god. He'd seen the footage with the people jumping. What kind of parent exposed their kid to that?

Pouf! The tower came down.

It was suddenly hard to breathe. Rage rose and grief clenched. I was a lightning rod, emotions zapping through me. I felt tall, stretched between earth and sky. I was Justice, eyes flashing as I spoke to his parents through clenched teeth. I was . . .

I forced myself to take a gulp of air, to feel my feet on the ground, to be in my body, in my classroom. His mother was a CPA and his father in finance. They knew people who had died. I understood why they watched the news. I continued to breathe. Slowly I realized eight faces had turned my way, eight mouths had formed little *O*'s. Thomas was still focused on the tower he was building. *Pouf!*

Oh. *Oh. Oh!* I remembered how calm they were yesterday when the head of school had come to talk with them about the new safety rules. *Only go outside with your teacher. Walk to your car with a parent or an adult.* They had been *fine,* dry-eyed, nodding seriously about "bad people" and needing to be more careful, at least for a little while.

I wasn't a lightning rod.

I was a radio transmitter.

A throbbing, grieving, raging transmitter. The faces turned toward mine were mirrors. What they were showing me wasn't theirs; it was mine.

Another deep breath. I closed my eyes. I envisioned reeling it all back in, the threads of grief and rage, the silks of confusion and sadness, the spiral of unfettered emotions. I reeled it all in.

I had to figure out how to ingest this, to compost this, to spin something new. Not just for myself, but for all of them.

———————

Of course, I took it to Gail.

"Good. Now you know that you need to contain yourself," she said in a tone that clearly discouraged any drama.

She slid in another needle, barely a pinch, in the cleft between thumb and forefinger.

"Okay. I need to contain myself," I repeated, trying to be as matter-of-fact as she was. "How?"

"That's the question, isn't it," Gail said, her curly head bobbing as she palpated a point below my elbow. "Sounds like you did a decent job of it. Relax and remember what you did. Feel it in your body."

She dimmed the lights and was gone.

I swam in the in-between, quickly losing sight of my assignment. Instead, my consciousness fluttered around my physical self, searching for sensations and assigning them words: ache in left calf is *worry,* constriction in chest is *fear.* There was an almost compulsive quality to it: feelings, sensations in my body, *had* to be translated. Time passed . . . or didn't. Words swirled. I grabbed for them, fished them from the depths, and formed a sort of false prescience, a marriage of thought, feeling, and anxiety.

Surfacing from the needles, I told Gail:

This will not be a bloodless coup.
I feel the catheter in my arm.
Giving or taking, I know not which.

I hope she rolled her eyes. She should have rolled her eyes. My "I am the oracle" phase was a bit much. Was I talking about learning to contain myself? About the knife-edge of war on which my country was pirouetting? I kept trying to find language to match the tumult in my mind, the feelings roiling through my body. It was a losing battle with melodrama. As I look back, it's clear that Gail wanted me to work on how to modulate my own energy: the moods and emotions I was transmitting to my class. But I was fixated on what was coming in, with honing what I was beginning to see as a secret superpower: my intuition. I wanted desperately to be the storybook person who had the previously unacknowledged gift that would, once recognized, save us all. This sort of plot twist would help me understand why I always ended up feeling like an outsider or an outcast: it wasn't because I was damaged but because I was gifted! It was like I was waiting for someone to say *oh, that's because you're magical, dear. We magical folks are always misunderstood, but we're so necessary for keeping the balance!* (And then I'd be sworn in to a secret society that predicted major weather events and the takeover attempts of hostile dictators.)

But Gail obviously hadn't read the script. She said, rather anticlimactically, "Your only job is to observe your thoughts. That's it. Observe."

They say savasana is the hardest pose in yoga—the relaxing, the letting go. How do you lie on the earth with your arms relaxed and open to the sky when you aren't in the safe lavender-scented space of the yoga studio?

I wish I could tell you I progressed in a straight line, doing each lesson only once, but my learning has always tended toward curlicues and spirals. Over the months to come I repeated the same lesson over and over, trying to understand both the song of stillness and the language of living with my whole being.

26

Breathe in red for the root chakra, exhale ooo.

Breathe in orange for the sacral, exhale ooh.

Breathe in yellow for the solar plexus, exhale aaw.

Breathe in green for the heart, exhale ahh.

Breathe in blue for the throat, exhale ehh.

Breathe in purple for the third eye, exhale ihh.

Breathe in indigo for the crown, exhale eee.

It was cold on the front stoop at 5 a.m., winter waiting behind autumn's crisp facade. I'd dragged the down comforter from my bed and was wrapped snug, the edges of the blanket tucked under my toes. There was no one about; the moon was absent. A streetlamp a few houses down gave just enough light that I could see Mrs. Cahill's cat stalking past her viburnum. In spring, the bush had big white snowball flowers. Now it was covered in limp colorless leaves, limned silver.

I was sitting out on the predawn stoop with only an aloof cat for company trying to hone my intuition. The stoop was still, a womb, a sacred space. There was no distraction. To begin, I practiced a breathing exercise I'd learned to activate each chakra. Eyes closed, I breathed in, visualizing the chakra's color, and breathed out, intoning (very quietly!) its vowel sound.

Annette and I were supposed to meet her boyfriend later that day in the Islamic rooms at the Met. But the night before, New York's mayor had said that he was going to close the city when the United States attacked Afghanistan . . . which was a day not being divulged to the public, although every newscaster had a sure date confirmed by an anonymous source. I didn't want to be stuck in town for days. So was today the day? Should I head downtown or not?

Done intoning, I checked in with my body, noting what was tight, what ached, what was relaxed. Then I imagined widening my senses, an aperture opening to take in the currents. I sat for a while, trying to just feel, attempting not to think.

Afghanistan, my brain began.

Shh! I responded.

I sat a little while longer.

Cold, my brain tried.

I know! I growled.

Then thirty-seven seconds of stillness. Realizing it might be all I got, I took stock of my body. What had changed within me during my outward scrying?

I started at my toes, sweeping my awareness upward and feeling for changes. My ankles felt like ankles, and my calves were my calves. Traveling up, I noticed a dull ache in my spine, near my waist, but that was pretty much always there. Up, up, up. Here, this was new: a tightness in my rib cage, like I was holding my breath; a slight constriction at the base of my throat.

Okay.

But what did it mean?

Sighing, I opened my eyes. The cat was now rhythmically licking a paw, perched on the cement steps that teetered up from the street.

"Well?" I asked it. It paused its cleaning to eye me before resuming its work. "You're no help," I grumbled, untangling myself from the blanket. Standing, I searched for the moon, but she was nowhere in sight.

The coffee maker spurted and blurted. It was late. I'd fallen back to sleep after my predawn meditations. *Coffee!* I jiggered impatiently, ready to replace the carafe with my cup. Annette raised an eyebrow. I stilled, leaning my elbows on the island.

"So?" she questioned. "What's the verdict? You coming?" She reached behind her to pull down two clean mugs, taking yesterday's, which I was about to reuse, and putting it in the sink. Quinn was at her boyfriend's for the night. No mug for her.

"I'm not sure. It doesn't feel quite right."

I wanted to go. Out of curiosity, to bear witness. Because New York still felt like my city. But it was Sunday. If I got stuck, I wouldn't make it to school on Monday. Annette worked downtown and would sleep at her boyfriend's anyway, so stuck wasn't a problem for her.

"Let's put on our city clothes and see how we feel," Annette suggested.

Dressed in my box-toed boots and cropped pants, I fished my tapestry coat out of the closet. I still wasn't certain.

I drove us down the hill to the train station. As we were pulling in, I made my choice. Instead of parking, I chauffeured Annette to the drop-off.

"I'm gonna pass," I told her.

"Yeah?" she checked.

"Yeah," I said firmly.

"Okay!" She leaned over to kiss my cheek, grabbing her square leather tote from the back, and headed for the platform, wrapping her crimson scarf around her neck as she walked. The Hudson was a silver-gray snake just beyond the tracks. I sat in the car and watched the train pull in. Annette, in her belted coat, got into the third car, then the train pulled out.

I sat for a bit, thinking. Maybe I'd do the Dennings Point Loop or find the back way up Mount Beacon. But that meant going home and changing into hiking clothes.

I sat for a few more minutes. The platform had emptied. The cars doing drop-offs were gone. The river beckoned. I glanced across it, eyeing the mountains in the distance. *Yeeeessss.* The Catskills. That felt right. With my mind made up, I put the car in gear.

At 12:40 the radio announced that we had attacked Afghanistan. I felt a little light-headed. This war was beyond misguided, but in that moment, as horrible as it sounds, I was relieved: if we had attacked Afghanistan, then my intuition was working.

The road into Woodstock was wooded, dotted with diners and tourist shops until, on the outskirts of town, trees gave way to Craftsman cottages and old farmhouses. I found myself craning my neck, trying to peer behind garden gates and up at the bric-a-brac of a well-restored turn-of-the-century home. After nearly hitting the car in front of Rosie as I looked everywhere but the road, it became apparent I would be wiser to explore on foot.

The first public lot was across from a farmers market, which seemed to be wrapping up. Still, I was able to grab a gluten-free muffin from a woman whose booth was only half packed.

A lanky guy in a tie-dyed T-shirt came through pushing a wheelbarrow full of drums: congas, bongos, tambourines, and bodhrans filled the space where mulch and a shovel would normally be. I took the last bite of muffin, licking brown sugar crumbs from my finger. It was such a bizarre juxtaposition—the drums and the rusty red wheelbarrow. I followed along, trying to look like I just happened to be going the same way.

A young family, boy perched on his father's shoulders, seemed to have the same plan, as did a few couples who'd been wandering the farmers market as it closed down. We all tried to look casual as we followed our pied piper. He rolled into an open square, which I immediately dubbed "the village green," and started handing out his cargo. Some looked prepared, like they'd come knowing there was going to be a wheelbarrow rolled in and drums passed out, while others looked bemused as the lanky guy fished out just the right instrument for each person, sometimes changing his mind right before the handoff. I stood on the outskirts, watching the drum circle organize and find its beat. People flowed toward the square; teenagers with locs, frayed jeans, and hippie skirts; tidy tourists clutching coffees; honeymooners holding hands. The throbbing rhythm intensified as locals arrived, bringing their own noisemakers. Shoes were discarded; dancers kept the beat with their feet. I could feel the bass in my heart, in my hips. It was overwhelming.

I slipped away, onto a narrow lane lined with cottages painted pearl pinks and sunset blues. The street dead-ended, but there was a little bridge that carried me to the next tiny lane. The drumming was still vibrating on the edge of my consciousness as I made my way up the little roads, stopping to study a shed with sea-glass wind chimes dangling from its eaves and an exuberant passionflower vine on a trellis made from rough-cut branches—I had thought passionflower was a southern plant.

Somehow I'd circled back to the main road. I wasn't one-hundred-percent sure where I was in relation to the parking lot, so I turned left at random. Across the street was a farmhouse. A sign said *Books & Gifts.* I smiled. Crossing the street, I climbed the steps to the front porch and went inside.

A little chime announced my presence. A woman behind a case of jewelry and crystals looked up, offered a beneficent smile, and said, "Welcome." New Age music purred through the speakers. *Oh shit,* I thought. *I hate these places.* The incense made my throat scratchy, and the books made my eyeballs itch. *Just a quick look around so I don't seem rude,* I decided, eyeing an easy route through the store. Choosing a stately pace (so polite!), I began my circle, pausing to pick things up and study them with what I hoped looked like interest.

When I reached the far corner, a petite woman appeared in the doorway of an adjacent room. Over her shoulder, I could see a shabby-chic love seat and an oval coffee table set with candles.

"Come," she offered. "Let me read your cards!" It must have been obvious I was looking to escape because she added, "It's on the house today."

I could feel the woman at the front counter watching, assessing. In my mind, she said smugly, *I knew you didn't belong here! Your aura's all off.* And suddenly I desperately wanted her acceptance. Shaking my head at myself, I took a fortifying breath, walked into the little room, and sat on the moss-colored couch.

The card reader took a seat across from me. She was dressed in slouchy jeans, her fox-colored hair casually piled on top of her head. Out in the store,

I'd thought she looked around my age. But up close her laugh lines said she was at least a decade older.

She smiled at me and gestured to the deck on the table between us. I picked it up and started through my routine: *shuffle, shuffle, shuffle.*

Her hands came down on mine, stilling them.

"What is it you want to know today?" she asked.

What do I want to know? I have no idea! I've just been herded into a reading. I wet my lips, preparing to speak, but she shook her head.

"Don't tell me. Tell the cards," she instructed, closing my hands around the deck.

Tell the cards? What? Confused, I glanced up at her.

"Just think about what you want to know while you hold the cards," she encouraged.

Um, okay. Rearranging the deck so the cards sat comfortably in my hands, I closed my eyes. Thoughts zinged around my brain. There was so much I wanted to know. I took a deep breath, and miraculously, my thoughts settled. In that quietude, I chose the simplest query: *What do I need to know right now?* I aimed the question at the cards and felt an electric sensation, like a gentle version of pins and needles, spreading across my palms. In surprise, I opened my eyes. The woman across from me smiled, her eyes crinkling.

"Now shuffle," she suggested.

My takeout chai went in the cup holder and the books I'd bought got tucked into the passenger seat (*Twelve Wild Swans* by Starhawk, *Shape Shifters: Shaman Women in Contemporary Society* by Michele Jamal, *Owning Your Own Shadow* by Robert Johnson, and *Drawing Down the Moon* by Margot Adler). I'd had dinner at an Indian restaurant, thumbing through my new reads over lamb vindaloo. Now it was getting dark, and I was very ready to be home.

Rosie purred to life. I flipped on the headlights, then pulled out of the lot. Purposefully, I left the radio off. In my mind, I pulled up the cards from my tarot reading: the Fool, the Hierophant, the Hanged Man, Ten of Wands, King of Swords, Prince of Cups. When the fox-haired woman laid down the King, she had asked me about my father, if we were having any issues. In the moment, I couldn't think of anything relevant. But now, I was remembering last night's dream.

In it, I was talking with Dad. He said, *I expect you to have Saddam Hussein tied and unconscious on the couch by the time I return.* I'd been hearing Saddam Hussein's name repeatedly in the weeks since 9/11, so it had been no surprise to me that he'd turned up in dreamland. I'd written off the dream as my mind processing current events. But thinking about it now, I focused on my dad, on the expectation that I could do this near-impossible thing, on the thought that I hadn't lived up to my father's expectations. I was supposed to become a lawyer. I was supposed to be straight. I was supposed to live in a nice house in the suburbs and have 1.5 kids who played behind a white picket fence. If all facets of a dream represent some part of the dreamer, maybe I was using my dad as a symbol for my own over-the-top expectations. Did I think that I could somehow be useful in stopping the war my country was starting? Those were some extravagant expectations.

In the *Shape Shifters* book I'd browsed over dinner, there was an essay by a voodoo priestess. She explained that when you go for training in voodoo, the priest or priestess will ask the gods *whose child is this?* The question is a way of learning to which voodoo *loa* the initiate will be attached. The question had churned up a longing in me, a loneliness. I couldn't turn to the parents of my birth to help me understand who I was becoming. *Whose child was I? Who would claim me?* Tears pricked my eyes.

Blinking, I flipped on the radio, searching for a news update. Station after station, the announcers' voices came through strident and overzealous. A feeling that had started earlier—a sort of heavy nausea pinging between my stomach and throat—began again. It wasn't physical; I didn't need to vomit. The sensation stretched, an energetic queasiness climbing to my crown and descending to my core.

Just before the turn onto I-87, something darted across the road. In the headlights, it was a void—small like a bird, scurrying like a squirrel. The car should have hit it, but I felt nothing. It was too featureless to be of this world. A slice of shadow or a sliver of starless night. I shivered and pushed *August and Everything After* into the CD player, turning the volume up louder than my churning thoughts.

27

Edges of old maps were decorated with mythical sea monsters, reminding us that between the reality we share and the void beyond lie roiling waters of change and creativity. This is where you begin to understand this thing called magic. But if you hope to also be a part of the modern world—to enjoy your lattes from Starbucks and the latest Netflix offering, the deeps are a place to visit, not a place to linger.

The year was in its final descent. I didn't know then how our psyches follow the seasons, how our souls lean into the darkness, naturally turning toward the inner realms.

I know now.

I know that when we unwind willingly, going to ground like a leaf or small animal, the downward spiral becomes a return to self, a centering.

But when we are unaware? When the darkness is uninvited? That's another story. Maybe it is one you know. If so, my tumble into the gloaming won't surprise you.

It happened in stages, a slow spiraling that started in the weeks just before Halloween. The world seemed full of menace as the denizens of my own underworld—anxiety, paranoia, and a desperate need to be important—all came out to play.

What were the early warning signs? Perhaps it was the shadows I seemed to see gathering, lurking in corners, or scurrying through the trees like a piece of the night. The evening I drove home from Woodstock was the first, but not the only, time I had dark visions. Maybe those sightings were intuition made visual or, perhaps, just my imagination run amok. Maybe the real beginning was the evening I heard about the anthrax attack in the subway.

After seeing Gail, I'd driven out Route 301 toward Fahnestock State Park. Driving is, still, my favorite meditative technique.

When I got to Canopus Lake, I pulled over in the empty gravel lot. The sun was low on the horizon, half hidden by puffy, luminous clouds. Rosie's hood was warm when I climbed onto it. The sun set as I leaned against the windshield, staring at the horizon as the night rushed toward the last lines of gold. This was where Quinn had been camping on one particularly stormy night before moving in with me. I hadn't known her well then but had called to invite her to sleep over. It seemed silly not to: there was plenty of space. When she arrived, her dark hair windblown and wet, I offered dinner. She told me she'd had an avocado. This was followed by an ode to avocados, the perfect self-contained, no-cook camping food. So now Fahnestock made me think not only of Quinn but also of avocados. And that reminded me I should get home. We'd planned a "family" dinner.

Climbing off the hood, I hopped into the driver's seat and turned on the engine. The late-October sky had inched toward inky indigo, so I flipped on the headlights. The road wound in broad sweeps toward Cold Spring. I swayed with the turns, smiling to myself. The radio was on low, a soft hum in the background.

Into this quiet dropped the words *breaking news*. I turned up the radio. "Nine people taken to the hospital from the Washington Heights subway station."

I'd been waiting for something like this.

Over breakfast I'd thought *something is going to happen tonight.* Sipping my coffee, I'd analyzed the voice in my head. It seemed to be in my mind. I couldn't find a source in my body. It was just a random, if rather insistent, thought. I decided it was anxiety speaking. But the words came again later, as I called the kids in from recess, and yet again when I was fishing in my bag for my car keys to drive to Gail's. Maybe it wasn't anxiety.

It put me in a space I had come to think of as the in-between: the mental holding pattern I would slip into as I waited to see if an intuitive hit would materialize. The in-between can simply be a waiting space, or it can be heavy—a place of helplessness, vague dread, and churning guilt. In this instance, it was the latter: I wanted to be right, even if right meant *something bad is going to happen tonight.* If something bad were going to happen, I couldn't do anything about it. My psyche was tuned to disaster radio and all I could do was listen. This was before I understood that *I* set the radio station, that I choose what my intuition attunes to. I now tune out these types of insights. They're a neat party trick, but don't ultimately lead to a joyful life. But that was a later realization. At this point, I was still learning, still floundering in the drama of it all.

The weeks since 9/11 had been chock-full of scares: bomb threats on bridges, terrorist updates, and anthrax alerts—because someone had realized they could send bacteria spores through the mail. A few days before, there had been two cases of anthrax in Florida; that morning a baby, the son of an ABC producer, was also diagnosed with the disease. The George Washington Bridge was still closed due to a bomb threat. The government had instituted a terrorist alert system, and it seemed permanently set to screaming red. It was not the best time to be learning to tune in to something greater than individual consciousness. The current collective was a lover's knot of anger and fear.

The next day, driving to work, I listened for updates on the subway story. *How were the people who'd been taken to the hospital? Was the subway line closed?*

I found no news. So, while the kids were at lunch, I searched the internet. Finally, I found it: the story I'd heard the day before—that nine were taken to the hospital from the Washington Heights subway station—had been "prematurely reported."

There was no anthrax, no bomb, no nothing.

I sat in front of the computer, stunned and furious. My ego, my sense of self, my overstretched anxiety, had all gotten tangled in this. Hot magma was pushing up from my core. I wanted to open my mouth and let it pour out in a never-ending stream. Through the wall, I could hear Joanne lecturing in the classroom next door, the words were unclear but the cadence reminded me that I was at work, that the kids would be back soon. I tried to modulate my response, to keep my feelings to myself. My head felt light; I realized I wasn't breathing.

With the distance of decades, it now sounds like an absurd overreaction. Yet I can remember the sensations in my body—the feeling of barely hanging on to control as the internal bombs detonated, the sense of flinging myself over the edge, not with the controlled step of the tarot deck's Fool, but instead diving, headlong and heedless, into the abyss.

I don't know how I got through the afternoon. My journal assures me it was a bad teacher day: *everything I said to the kids was wrong, wrong, wrong.* And that makes sense, since my body was in the classroom, but my psyche was in the deeps and, as the maps warned, there were monsters there. They stoked the fires in my core until I didn't even remember what exactly I was angry about. I only knew I was burning.

By the time I climbed in the car to drive home, I was wicking rage. I'd been played by fate. Worse, I'd been telling myself this crazy-ass story: If there was magic and I learned to use it, then there was more to life than the human rat race. And, if there was more to life than the human rat race, then exploring what magic existed in the world actually was a meaningful pursuit. In the past few months, this quest had ignited a sense of purpose in me, an inner calm and sense of knowing what I was supposed to do with my life, a feeling I hadn't felt since I gave up riding horses. But it was all a crock. And Gail? Did she believe this hocus-pocus or was this financial, simply a way to keep me coming for appointments?

Even as I thought this, a part of me knew it wasn't true. In my journal, I immediately noted my shame even while writing down the thoughts. There was something so inherently good and grounded about Gail. You didn't need to be psychic to feel it. But in that moment, when there was a flash fire in my veins, all I could think was:

This is all bullshit. Maybe everything is bullshit.

I was slipping back and forth, pushed and pulled by the tide of my own emotions and the overwhelming amount of information I was trying to process, both in physical reality and in the spiritual spaces I was cultivating. Later, I would learn to create rules for myself, to slip into the deeps by choice, closing the way behind me to avoid this sort of slippage. But I had no rules for my psyche yet. I'd blown open the doors not realizing I'd ever need to close them again.

I was only a mile or so from school, cruising down a tree-lined road, neat fields visible through the branches. My mind, however, was far away. All my thoughts were of blood and rage. I could taste it in my mouth, feel the slickness on my tongue. Glancing in the rearview mirror, I saw my teeth sheeted with blood.

Wait. My teeth were sheeted with blood.

I looked in the mirror again, suddenly present to myself. Up ahead, the verge widened enough to pull over. Turning on my blinker, I slid the car under a canopy of vermillion leaves.

Grabbing the rearview mirror, I swiveled it toward me and pulled back my lips. My teeth *were* pink, even red-streaked where the blood still flowed. My tongue was slick and coppery. Closing my eyes, I tipped back against the headrest.

Inhale. Exhale. I coached myself. I let go of the gnashing and gashing in my mind.

Inhale. Exhale. I released the patina of scarlet that was burnishing my thoughts and pushed the bloody images out with my breath. I pulled in golden light, consciously painting my eyelids with sunshine.

When I felt calmer, I fished a tissue from my bag and dabbed my teeth. Part of me thought the tissue would remain pristine, that I had imagined the whole thing.

I looked down. In my hand, the tissue was splotched pink.

———————

Since the abortion, I'd been making a study of how my feelings, as well as input from the world around me, affected my body. September 11 happened not long after I'd begun this process. I would notice how someone else's emotions could cause a stomachache, or an impending storm would make my head tighten. I'd been weaving myself into the web of the world, feeling less isolated and more a part of. But now I realized I had seen myself as merely a strand, responsive to everything from the wind to the insects vibrating the weaving. I'd imagined myself as having no agency on this world web.

I remembered the day right after 9/11 when the class had broken down, their grief and anguish a response to my own. While I'd spent time honing the skills of intuition, I hadn't really contemplated the yang to that yin: how my own emotions and thoughts could materialize, and become physical. How something could move from the inside of the self to the outside. This was a different kind of birthing.

Gail's admonition to simply observe took on new weight.

As I pulled back onto the road, I considered how to make my mind still, to leave the monsters to the depths unless I consciously called them up. While Gail could be a guide and an anchor, ultimately, I would need to learn to sail these seas myself.

———————

When I got home that day, I drew a tarot card. Just one, for guidance. The Two of Wands. A man stands on a rampart but instead of taking in the vista, he stares at a small globe that rests on his palm. The real world is stretched out before him, but his focus is on the world in his hand.

I didn't pull out the little booklet. The guidance was obvious: I had to see both the "real" world around me and the internal worlds within. They were mirrors of each other: microcosm and macrocosm.

28

Halloween costumes are a modern take on an ancient tradition: In Celtic cultures, it was known that, at this time of year, the world of the living and that of the dead drew close to each other. Costumes, often of animals, were worn to discourage the dead from recognizing the living, thus keeping unwanted visitations to a minimum.

Something kept niggling me, a thing that had nothing to do with anthrax and bomb threats. Or maybe it did, in a sideways sort of way. One evening, during my senior year in college, I had been curled in my roommate's leather club chair, binge-watching American Movie Classics. Since freshman year, Katharine Hepburn's dry wit had gotten me through final exam week.

I was home alone this particular evening, wrapped in a blanket to ward off Michigan's chill. On the screen, a black-and-white Kate paddled near the edge of a swimming pool, her chiseled cheeks prominent under a bathing cap. She was trying to capture the essence of the word *yare* for a nonsailor:

It means ... oh, what does it mean? Easy to handle, quick to the helm. Fast. Right. Everything a boat should be ...

The image flickered. I felt a presence beside me and glanced over my shoulder, skin prickling. Not with fear exactly; more with awareness. But there was nothing visible. That's when I did an odd thing: instead of turning back to the TV, I lifted my chin, as if to be kissed. Sure enough, I felt lips press mine. I sensed *goodbye* and a drawing away. Tears rolled down my cheeks. Hepburn carried on in the background as I sat, stunned, staring at empty air. Just for a second, I'd seen a man. Dark hair, cheeks chiseled like hers, not terribly tall. He was in uniform—khaki jacket, crisp and belted. I didn't recognize him, but he looked so wistful, reaching for my chin. And then he was gone.

Maybe it was seeing the uniforms again, on TV every evening like they had been during the Gulf War, that brought the memory back. Halloween was fast approaching, and according to the books I'd been reading, the veil between the world of those living and those passed was thin at this time of year. Maybe I could contact him. See who he was and why he'd come.

That was my plan as I arrived home, hauling my schoolbag, now laden with Halloween candy from CVS. I was looking forward to sorting through the Hershey's miniatures and pulling out the Special Dark before putting the rest in a bowl by the door. Gail had me on a sugar-free diet. She said sugar activated the Earth element and grounded the psyche. That's why she gave me a square of chocolate when the needles made me loopy—to bring me back down. But I deserved a little seasonal sweetness, I'd decided, as I hefted the bag up the steps to the porch.

Putting down my haul to unlock the door, I felt a chill, a sense of trepidation. I froze, then glanced left and right. No one was on the street. Nothing moved but the mostly dead leaves of the Russian sage, which rattled in the breeze. I looked around again, eyeing the dilapidated garage. Nothing. Closing my eyes, I *felt* around. There was a light crawling up my spine. The sensation of being watched, perhaps?

On instinct, I picked up two smooth stones Quinn had unearthed when she was digging in the garden. Each was as big as my spread hand. They'd been sitting on the porch since spring. Holding the stones, I called upon the guardians of the house—I didn't overthink it; I just decided the house had guardians—and asked them to protect all within, to let no evil pass. The request rolled out in rhyme, years of poetry-training tripping off my tongue. Eyes closed, I waited until I felt a zing of confirmation in my hands—a sensation I'd been attuned to since the card reading in Woodstock, when it had felt like the cards were saying *yes*. Now I had the same sensation from the rocks. Zing acquired and "spell" complete, I placed the stones on either side of the steps and headed in to get ready for trick-or-treaters.

After putting the candy in a bowl, sans dark chocolate, I pulled out salt and four votive candles. I hadn't previously felt the urge to use the traditional stuff of ritual, but tonight it seemed right. Candles to light the four directions, salt to cast the circle.

Quinn was doing Halloween with her boyfriend and his kids, and Annette rarely made it home before eight o'clock, so I had to figure out how to do my ritual while still being available to hand out candy. Maybe a protection circle existed more in liminal space than in physical space? Maybe I could think of it not as a circle on the ground but more like a circle around myself, a sacred space I could carry with me?

The doorbell chimed. It was early, not yet five o'clock. I padded down the hall with the bowl of candy. Through the sheer curtain I saw the scarlet flash of a baseball cap. It was such a relief not to have the solid steel door anymore! A friend had helped me install the carved double doors we'd found at an architectural salvage yard. We'd stripped a hundred years of paint, treated the heart of pine underneath with tung oil, and then given them a silky coat of wax. The brass knob was engraved with vines and felt weighty as I twisted it. *Who knew a door could give me such pleasure?* I pondered, running a hand up the wood as I opened it.

On the porch, Mikey, who lived down the street with his aunt and uncle, grinned at me, no costume in sight. I could tell the smile was meant to be sweet, but sweet was not in his thirteen-year-old repertoire. Sarcastic, witty, whip-smart: yes. Sweet: no.

"Trick or treat!" he chimed, holding out a hand.

"Trick!" I replied promptly. I leaned against the doorframe, the bowl of candy cradled in front of me. "You're not in costume." He tried to reach in, but I twisted away.

His eyes widened. "But, Em!" he wheedled. His uncle had swung by earlier, making me promise to give the kid a hard time for refusing to dress up. Apparently, this year he'd decided he was too mature for a costume—though not, apparently, too old for treats.

"I'll tell you what," I bargained. "Tell me the story of that Gothic mansion on Craig House Lane and you can have three pieces of candy." I knew the neighborhood kids rode their bikes over there sometimes, cruising past the no-trespassing signs that had appeared when the house had been closed up last year. The mansion was on my long-walk loop. More than once, I'd seen their bikes by the locked gate. It was a gate I'd been known to push my face against as I tried to catch a glimpse beyond the overgrown trees and straggly roses. It seemed almost romantic: a brick Gothic Revival on a winding little lane in a rolling neighborhood near the Hudson. Except pushing my face against the gate made me feel nauseous. My vision would gray a bit, the way it does when the sun ducks behind a cloud, cooling all the colors.

But Mikey didn't seem put off by whatever I sensed there. His eyes lit up. "That place is so cool! There's a hole in the back...."

"La, la, la, la, la, la!" I sang out. "Don't tell me about the breaking-and-entering stuff, dude!"

He looked at the ground, grinning at me from under his lashes. We both laughed.

"Seriously, Em. It's cool and kind of creepy. It's huge and there's this giant organ inside, the kind with the pipes, like at church."

A giant pipe organ? In a house? Curiouser and curiouser.

"Know anything about its history?" I prompted.

"Oh yeah! It was a place for crazy people! The exercise lady's mom was there, and she jumped off the roof and died!"

The exercise lady?

Later, I would get curious. Turns out "the exercise lady's mom" was Frances Seymour, wife of Henry Fonda and mother to Jane. Zelda Fitzgerald had also been a patient there, as well as Rosemary Kennedy. The pipe organ and the music room were designed by the famous architect Richard Morris Hunt.

But I knew none of this at the time. What I did know was that Mikey had earned a bit of Halloween candy, so I held out the bowl. Mikey pulled it close and fished out three Krackels.

"Thanks, Em!" he hollered over his shoulder as he grabbed his bike from the sidewalk.

Bemused, I went back inside. I was grateful for the guardian stones I'd set by the steps. This town had plenty of ghosts.

———————

The square room in the front of the house, the one with the bay window, felt best for the ritual. Facing west, I could see the last licks of light limning my neighbor's roof. I imagined the sun setting over the river beyond the houses.

As I gathered the supplies from the kitchen, I wondered who I was becoming. Yesterday I had told a friend's grandson I was a witch. I'd said it because it was almost Halloween, and he was a kid who needed a little real-world magic. Was it a lie? The beginning of a truth?

I placed candles in the cardinal directions. The house faced due west, which made it easy to pick out the compass points. That was the simple part. I'd read about casting a circle but never tried it. Should I write down what I was going to say? There was no way I was reading something from a book: that would feel like synagogue. Standing in the center of the circle, I turned toward each direction, socks sliding on the wood floor. My mind was blank. I definitely needed to write something down. My journal, the one with the repeating blue cranes, was on the sofa. As I searched for a pen, I wondered if rhyming was simply cliché, or was it cliché because it had its own power? Rhyme and rhythm turned words into chant, and chant was used traditionally in prayers and rituals. So maybe rhyming was a technique for separating the language of power from the language of everyday life. Maybe it was a way to focus energy and intent. I considered this and decided to build up to the rhyme so that it became the key in the lock, activating the circle.

Experimenting, I wrote:

> *I call upon the north*
> *earth and cool, starred winter night, hibernation close.*
> *I bring you warmth.*
>
> *I call upon the east.*
> *Mountains, dawn sun, morning haze.*
> *I bring you breath.*
>
> *I call upon the south.*
> *Clear noon, bright, and fire-eyed.*
> *I match your flame.*
>
> *I call upon the west.*
> *Setting sun, river always knowing.*
> *I bring the twins of ebb and flow.*
>
> *I call on the north to close the cast,*
> *to seal with salt this circle round.*
> *Sky above and earth below, form a sphere:*
> *none may enter, none may go.*

Then I planned to move to the center of the circle, where I had placed a meditation cushion.

> *I call to those who have guided me, who choose to guide me now.*
> *On this night when veils are thin, I ask the soul who knew me when:*
> *join my circle for a time, live again within my mind.*

The doorbell rang twice while I was writing. Distracted, I handed out treats.

I looked over my words. It felt like they were weaving me in, making me a part of the web of the elements. It was like I was creating the little orb from the Two of Wands card, but instead of cradling it, it would cradle me.

I wish I could tell you my ritual banged doors and fluttered curtains, or that this was the moment I finally lit a candle with my mind. Or even that the spirit of the soldier joined me and explained our deep cosmic connection. But that's not what happened. Nothing happened—at least not that I could sense. Still, something in me quieted. I felt centered and full. Miraculously, I hadn't been disturbed.

When the ritual was done, I sat on the stoop, one step up from the guardian stones, and handed out the rest of the candy. The moon was full. The Hunter's Moon. Diana's moon. I hadn't known all the full moons had names: I thought it was only special ones, like the Strawberry Moon, whose name I learned from a childhood story. Quinn knew all the names; it felt like hidden knowledge, even though it was available in every Farmers' Almanac. I wanted to learn, too, to be able to call the moons by name.

While I was sitting outside, Annette came home, a bit of Manhattan striding down our sleepy-town street in her black trench coat. She snagged the last two pieces of chocolate from my bowl and ate them while lounging with me on the steps. After she licked her fingers and tossed the balled-up wrappers into the bowl, we headed inside. She hung up her coat and changed into slippers, while I boiled water for tea.

"What ritual were you doing?" Annette called as she passed through the front hall to join me in the kitchen. I told her about casting a circle and the soldier boy I'd never known. We drank tea made from the dried leaves of the peppermint and spearmint Quinn had grown in the garden. The honey was local and so sweet, I needed only a dab. Stillness rested within me, a deep mountain lake, a forgotten sea.

Before bed, Annette and I huddled together to draw one card to guide us through the night of roving spirits.

We pulled the Hierophant, reversed.

Upright, this card speaks to religious initiation and walking the known path. But inverted, it's instead about making one's own way to the sacred. Either way—right side up or upside down—two keys cross the Hierophant's chest.

Keys unlock doors: the doors to the mysteries of esoteric wisdom and knowledge, the doors to the conscious and subconscious, the doors that were shut long ago to lock my inner witch up tight. It seemed appropriate on Halloween night to fit the key into the lock and give it a twist.

29

For stomachaches and other anxieties: Grate two inches of fresh ginger into a saucepan. Add water. Simmer for twenty minutes. Strain. Add honey and lime to taste.

It was the week before Thanksgiving break. A very long week. Constantly observing what my body felt, paired with the emotional monitoring, was exhausting. And at school, Paula, one of my students, was falling apart. She'd started eating things: She began by gnawing on pencils and pens, then she moved on to her shirtfront, pulling the neck up into her mouth. Yesterday it had been a plastic bag. Even when she seemed fine, her presence was a constant weight behind my eyeballs, a pressure like unshed tears. My concern bounced off the school's administrators. While I heard my voice, calm and professional, reporting the plastic bag incident, the words became a banshee's howl in my mind. *She was EATING a PLASTIC baaaagggg!!!* Her distress swirled around me—a vortex, a transference. Over and over, I asked my inner voice, *What am I supposed to teach this child?* Over and over, I came up blank. The atmosphere at the school wasn't helping. The internal dramas were never-ending which made work a boot camp for practicing my boundaries. One boundary I had already set, if only in my mind, was that I would not be signing a contract for next year.

Luckily my intuition was improving; like a muscle that had just needed some strengthening, it was becoming increasingly reliable. Today I was picking names from a hat for a part in the Thanksgiving skit. As soon as I wrote Liam's name on the paper, I knew it would be him. His parents were so overbearing. It was easy to picture them at the postproduction party, twinkling about the brilliance of their little boy. Ugh. I thought about turning my will toward making it *not* him.

(*Could I do that? Would it work?*)

But I decided, since my motives were less than pure, I'd let it be. Liam's name was picked.

Eight p.m. rolled around but no one was home yet, despite it being *Buffy* night. I flipped on the TV and stretched out on the couch, half watching and half dozing. Tara was breaking up with Willow, staring earnestly into her eyes. Their faces were close, noses almost touching. The camera had zoomed in, silhouetting them against the candlelight.

The phone rang. I ignored it. Willow was begging Tara not to leave, promising not to do any more magic.

"I'll go a month without doing any magic. I won't do a single spell;
I swear!" Willow vowed.

I didn't believe her. And it looked like Tara didn't either. How do you swear off being who you are? Still, their conversation felt sort of familiar, which made me vaguely uncomfortable.

"Go a week—one week without magic . . ." Tara challenged.

Who had said something similar recently? I replayed the week backward, recalling random run-ins and coffee dates. Ah! It was a friend I knew from yoga. As a teacher at two well-known retreat centers, he'd seen many people spin out and become disconnected from their lives. *Nothing good comes from seeking or attaining this type of power.*

On-screen, Willow lasted about ten minutes before performing a spell to make Tara forget about the whole swearing-off-magic thing. And that's the line: manipulating other people. My dad once said to me, attempting to explain the legal concept of free will, *your free will ends where my nose begins.*

The phone rang again. I ignored it again.

But my friend from yoga had been talking about something different from Willow's on-screen manipulations. John had seen people step so wholly into the unseen that they lost the ability to live in the shared reality of this world, their behavior ranging from obsessive to wild to withdrawn. And he wasn't wrong. I remembered four days in college when I had floated in the hidden realms of my own mind, disconnected entirely from my body. When I reconnected with myself, I found my bedroom strewn with shopping bags and receipts for clothes I didn't remember buying. Notebooks and scrap paper were scrawled with words dredged up from elsewhere.

There was an edge. I'd almost fallen over it before, acting as the tarot's Fool, blasé as his stride lengthens, foot hanging over the void.

The phone rang for the third time. On the TV, only the final credits were left. As I reached for the receiver, my sister's name flashed through my mind.

"Can't a girl watch *Buffy* in peace?" I grumped.

"Is that any way to answer the phone?" she asked, immediately exasperated.

"I knew it was you," I said, standing to stretch. And I had known. With one-hundred-percent certainty. Where was the danger in that? What's the difference between tuning in and spinning out?

I sat back on the sofa while we talked. Eyes closed, I felt the nap of the couch's velvet, soft one way, nubby the other. We made plans for Thanksgiving. I'd arrive early to help my mom cook. The beach in November would be quiet, and I relished the thought of a few days of quiet food prep.

When we hung up, my fingers kept going: back and forth, back and forth. My stomach had been rhythmically clenching all day, and it felt like it was syncing with my fingers: *clench, clench, clench*. This sort of thing used to be simple: stomach cramps equaled bad sushi or menstruation. Now I wasn't sure what they meant. Was this sensation coming from within or without?

Ever since I was young, people have emptied their feelings into my lap, knowing I'll sort them out or at least ask the right questions so they can go through it themselves. It used to baffle my mom, the way her friends would chat with her twelve-year-old daughter. My fingers continued to trail back and forth over the velvet. *Smooth, coarse, smooth, coarse.* But how could I sort feelings and pick the right silk out of the tangle of the web, when I no longer knew what emotions were? Were they the things in your head or the things in your body? What was the difference between intuition and emotion? My belly clenched again. Was that real physical pain or a message from my inner knowing? How could I tell?

Quinn had asked me the other day why I was doing this to myself. By "this" I think she meant the experiments with intuition, the trying to understand the nonphysical messages my body received. Like John from yoga, she was concerned. She said I kept talking about "power." Having power, honing power.

"Power over what?" she asked. "What are you trying to learn?"

I think she was using *power* in the interpersonal or political sense, while for me it was something else. Maybe *qi* or *energy* would have been a better word for the thing I was trying to harness. Not just personal energy, but some larger force—cosmic qi.

That's the grand answer, the philosophical answer, the conscious-mind answer. But subconsciously I think I was trying to conquer a fear. Not a fear of magic or the occult or paranormal prowess. Instead, I was attempting to permanently disarm the part of myself that insisted magic couldn't exist outside a book, the skeptic who couldn't accept a magical worldview but also had an existential horror of living in "mundania," of knowing the world was without magic.

I went into the kitchen to make a cup of tea. As I leaned down to pull the saucepan from the lower cabinet, a needle of pain pierced my temple. Standing up, I rubbed at it as I searched the drawers for the grater. Annette didn't always put things away where I did. Not that I was complaining: because of her, we ate amazingly well at our Home for Wayward Women.

But I wasn't going to be eating anytime soon. My stomach roiled at the thought. The cooktop *click, click, click*ed as the gas came on. The water simmered, and I grated ginger directly into the pan, scattering ginger schmutz onto the cooktop. I licked my finger and touched the tip onto each little ginger bit to pick them up. My skull throbbed. I licked my finger again, and heat flooded my mouth.

By the time my tea was through steeping, I was well on my way to a full-blown migraine. The pungent scent of ginger wafted through the kitchen, making me nauseous. I retreated to the living room. A short time later, Annette and Quinn walked in together, Quinn yelling *we're home, honey!* I was huddled in a corner of the couch, shivering.

"No fever," Annette said, the back of her long fingers cool on my forehead. She moved behind me, working the muscles in my neck. The pain took a half step back. Quinn had pulled out lavender oil and was massaging my feet. Slowly, my muscles unclenched. The shaking stopped. Quinn brought warm water with lemon; I tried a few sips.

What kind of falling apart is this? I wondered, tucked into bed with candles lit on the windowsills and a heating pad on my belly. I felt ridiculously lucky for the friendship of these two women. We'd become attuned to each other's needs: cooked, lit candles, drew baths, procured tissues . . . little things that weren't so little. I never could have planned this when I bought the house: the coming together of the three of us. We each had our own dramas. Both Quinn and Annette were in tumultuous relationships. Annette was considering leaving her job. And me? I didn't have good words for what I was going through. Or *putting myself through* as they would have said.

I must have slept. When I woke, the candles were out. The clenching in my middle had barely eased, but the sheets were warm and sticky. *Oh!* I lay still, feeling my blood pumping. I was almost relieved. *This* was the anxiety, the pain. Then the fog of sleep rolled back enough for me to realize I was going to ruin the mattress. Hauling myself out of bed, I padded to the bathroom. The house was still. It was late—or early.

As quietly as I could, I filled the tub with hot water. The quarter moon was low in the sky, offering just enough light to see by. *Hello, Diana,* I thought. When I had been in France in college, I visited Île Saint-Honorat, which was a boat ride from the mainland. The clay-tiled tower of the monastery rose steadily out of the waters of the Côte d'Azur as the boat drew near. The island had housed a temple to Poseidon before coming under church ownership. In the courtyard was a statue of Diana, goddess of the moon and the hunt. I'd thought she was also the goddess who first bridled a horse, but Quinn told me I was remembering my Edith Hamilton incorrectly: the horse story was Athena's. Horses or no, I'd sat at Diana's feet for nearly an hour. It was she I had thought of when, as a teen in synagogue, I'd read *the Lord is One* and thought *No, he's not.*

Back then I had a voice inside me. It was old and calm, residing deep in my core. It would speak, and I would know what to do, what to say, what to write. It was as if a winsome goddess or ancient witch lived somewhere within me. I hadn't heard her words in a very long time, but it seemed, now, she whispered soothingly *Child.* I imagined her fingers stroking the hair back from my forehead, a small smile on her face as she shook her head in bemusement.

The moon—or Diana?—glinted through the window. Closing my eyes, I confessed my pain: the ache in my core, the grief in my heart, the confusion in my soul. Gathering the strands in my hands as if emotions were tangible, I held it up like an offering. My breath reached down to rise and fall in my bleeding belly.

The bathwater had cooled. "Please, take it all," I whispered and unplugged the drain.

30

In the far reaches of Siberia, where winter is cold and harsh, the longest night is lit by Mother Deer, who flies south and returns, the sun cradled in her antlers. This is the sky's story of the winter solstice. Earth has her own, and tells of the Greek goddess Persephone, who was abducted to the underworld. Both are death and rebirth stories, the type that have inspired humans for millennia.

On the night of the first snow, I dreamed of a deer—a tall stag with gold-tipped antlers. I was sorting the details of the dream while driving home from work. At a bend in the road, where the shorn fields changed to forest, a stag walked out of the woods, crossing in front of my car. He turned to look at me as he passed, his face mud-splattered, his coat winter-thick. Animals came fast after that: a red-shouldered hawk flying level with my car's window as I drove to my sister's, a barred owl swooping silently across our path as we carried groceries from the car.

There were often animals in my visions after Gail arranged her needles, but not these particular beasts. I wondered what it meant, but I didn't have time to ask at our next appointment; I was too concerned with getting instructions for parent/teacher conferences, figuring out how to keep parental energy from sticking to me and my energy from leaking onto them.

I was getting practical with what I was learning and beginning to apply to my everyday life. After reading about visualization last week I'd started imagining Paula woven back into the fabric of the class. In the morning before the students arrived and in the evening after they left, I would sit quietly, imagining each child as a thread. Amelia was indigo, Liam bright yellow, and Thomas a sea green. First, I laid the warp—the school itself, the classroom, the other teachers, me—the structures upon which the weaving depended.

Then I wove the children in, letting them form their own bright patterns. During the day, if Paula became what I thought of as a loose end, I called up the tapestry in my mind's eye and wove her back in. It only took a blink to imagine the reweaving. And maybe, somehow, it was helping. She seemed less ragged, more integrated. Or maybe the change came from following the advice of my teaching assistant who, I'd discovered, had been studying Wicca for years, despite being only twenty herself.

"Bounce her energy back to her," she suggested. "After she gets the rebound a few times, she'll change her behavior."

So I also carried an imaginary rubber shield and wore invisible rubber wristbands like Wonder Woman. If nothing else, the visualization restored my sense of humor.

My teaching assistant *saw* energy. She described it as colors and movement. While I didn't see anything like that, I was beginning to realize that I *felt* it. It might have been easier if I had seen it. Maybe, like her, I would have realized at a younger age that something unusual was going on. But when you feel energy, which I later learned was called *clairsentience,* it's pretty easy to think all the various sensations you encounter are your own aches and pains. Beginning to be able to sort the incoming data—to ask myself *is this mine?* so I could distinguish input from within versus input from without—was helping me understand what the twinges, crawling skin, and other flare-ups meant.

Despite feeling less like a loose end myself, I was still nervous about the conferences. Parents could be intense in myriad ways: protective, obtuse, ambitious. Now that I was aware how much my emotions radiated, I needed to keep myself in check. And I wouldn't be able to concentrate if I was spending the entire chat feeling where *their* emotions were landing in my body. I'd started eating sugar again, on purpose, to slow the barrage of extrasensory input. Sugar made me feel disconnected. I complained about it to Gail, knowing I sounded a bit like Goldilocks.

"But that's what you wanted, right? To feel a little less? So how about a reframe: you chose to disconnect. It's like turning the volume way down. And that's showing you that you have control." She slid a needle into my wrist. I liked those, they barely pinged. The toes were intense, and my calf muscle tightened as she palpated down my leg. Finding a point she liked, thankfully above the ankle, she pricked me with the final needle.

"Imagine creating a barrier between your energy and other people's," she said. "Try some different visualizations: maybe build a wall or put up a force field. Or"—she grinned—"imagine a bubble of air that hardens when something tries to get through. See what feels natural for you."

The lights dimmed and she was gone.

I don't remember what images I played with that day on Gail's table. Over the years I've tried many things: building a wall, stone by stone, which was an idea I'd gotten from Katherine Kurtz's novels; encasing myself in the bark of a tree; imagining a blinding brightness, like the heart of a supernova, that would *pfft* anything that tried to get through. For a while I used the image of a screen door, letting light and sound through but filtering out the bigger stuff. Now I use an imaginary hoodie—I zip myself in—or a little reverse-flow trick that works well for crowds: I push love outward so it's difficult for other energy to move against the current and flow toward me.

Whatever image I was experimenting with then, it seemed to work. My journal assures me that the conferences went well, that I didn't *"come home in an emotional twitter."* And when, later that week, I circumnavigated the site of the World Trade Center, I was able to stay in my own energetic space, the emotions exuded from mourners and tourists a gentle rustle at the edges of my consciousness.

The ruins rose like a cathedral, pointed arches falling sideways toward the sky. Letters and photos lined the streets by the harbor. Roses were woven into the tall construction fencing; when the breeze was right, their scent would waft across the crowds in a silent benediction, gently reminding me of the attar of wild roses that accompanied my midnight runs. Gail had told me that many got sick after visiting the site, but I felt somehow stronger. Quinn noticed, saying I seemed calmer, more poised. I think I found some peace in witnessing the destruction, as if seeing it in real life allowed my imagination to finally still.

And so the year wound down.

I'd read about a culture that believed the world died when the sun set on solstice eve. They said that the longest night was a void, a nothingness, a prayer for a new beginning. Despite many searches over the years, I've never been able to find this reference again. But it's stuck with me, lingering in my imagination. So as the winter solstice approached, I shared the story with Annette and Quinn. We decided to sit vigil through the longest night, to make sure the sun returned. A ritual formed organically. Before the sun set, we cut thin strips of paper and wrote what we would each let die with the death of the year. Then we lit the fire in a stone circle in the yard and sat telling tales of what we had lost and whom we had left behind in the year that was. As we shared, we burned the slips of paper, making sure they went to ash. We had invited a few friends. Everyone seemed ensconced in the ritual bubble, able to bring what they wanted and take what they needed. By dawn, we were loopy with lack of sleep, banging pots and pans to cheer on the sun as it rose above the horizon.

Sol-stice means *sun standing still*; the sun appears to remain in one place on the horizon for a few days before and after each solstice. So, while the sun had reached its southernmost point in the sky and had already swung around to head back north, I stayed in my moment of darkness for the length of the solstice, the time when the sun appears to stand still. Having finally touched the bottom of the well, I found that, instead of drowning, I was swimming in amniotic fluid, warm and waiting. This liminal space was heavy, but comforting, like snuggling under a pile of quilts. So, in the queen-size bed of winter, I paused to dream. Animals gathered. Each bore a gift as fleeting as thought. The questions I'd been asking swam past me: *Who am I? Who am I becoming?* In this dreamscape, entire countries coalesced, lands without name, mountains I had climbed and those that eluded me.

Gail entered the dreamscape. *Call yourself home,* she directed. *You're starting to lose pieces of yourself.*

But how could I call to those countless versions of myself who had been living separate lives in the swirling worlds of my mind? What could I offer to them? What kind of life was I creating?

I knew I didn't want to be the wild-eyed novitiate of the past year, swinging between extremes. And I could see now that there was a narcissism to measuring the world by my reaction to it.

And I was beginning to realize I needed to ground the power I'd found in a purpose. As Quinn and Annette had both asked: *Why was I doing this?* How could this knowledge serve a goddess grander than Melodrama? What was the secret to spinning this silk into the web of my daily living, so it was not something I did, but an expression of who I was? Maybe the mystical sects of the world's religions held a key. Perhaps hidden in their lore was a structure to the things I was discovering through experimentation.

As the days began to lengthen in incremental shifts, I looked up, up, up at the sky, to the dot I knew was the sun. It was time to feel its warmth on my skin again, to emerge from my dark womb of becoming. My toes found purchase on the loamy bottom, the deep earth of my well. I bent my knees and pushed upward, calling to all the parts of me to swim together toward the surface.

31

The modern concept of chakras evolved through the Vedic tradition, but many cultures have a theory of energy centers connecting our bodies to the outer world. When you let go of specifics and just feel, where does your inner world connect with the outer world? Can you feel the points of contact, the swirling doorways in and out of yourself?

Three long tapers were lit in the candelabra I'd placed on a wood crate in the bay window. As a New Year's gift to myself, I'd decided the ultimate luxury would be not just to get a massage but to have a massage therapist come to me. Quinn and Annette were both with their boyfriends, so I had the place to myself.

After hanging sheers over the bay window, I cleaned the front room and dragged in crates and side tables to perch candles upon. Pillars, tea lights, and tapers shimmered against the early evening glow. Upstairs, the claw-foot bathtub was scrubbed and waiting. Bath salts, my favorite towel (huge enough to wrap around me like a throw blanket), more candles, and a bottle of Shiraz were all set out. Takeout Chinese was waiting on the kitchen counter. Bliss.

The massage therapist arrived a few minutes early. She began setting up her table, shooing me upstairs to strip. I came down in a plaid flannel robe and flip-flops—there was still no going barefoot even though I'd had the floors sanded and refinished. The stairs randomly produced carpet tacks; I suspect they were hidden under the floorboards and the house occasionally scattered them to get my attention.

With the masseuse in the kitchen washing her hands, I dropped the robe and climbed onto the table's fresh sheets, fitting my face into the headrest. The scent of lavender and vanilla moved through the air, the sound of chanting came from the stereo. I let myself sink.

When I surfaced, I could feel her hand on my left shoulder. The shoulder felt . . . weak, somehow. And heavy. I felt sorry for it. It seemed so sad. Inadvertently, tears filled my eyes.

"What's going on here?" she asked, her voice soft and low.

"It feels . . . weak," I told her, letting my inner thoughts flow through my lips. "Sad? Can a shoulder feel sad?" I laughed a little, breaking the stillness.

"Do you know why?" she questioned, still quiet, reclaiming the bubble of Zen she had created around us. "Feel around. Do any other sensations go with the sad feeling?"

I didn't think, just spoke. "My ear hurts and my shoulder feels guilty."

"Guilty?"

"It dropped me. It feels bad because it dropped me." I suddenly saw the world upside down, felt the pinch of a metal rod under my knees. It was the jungle gym in my childhood backyard. I loved to hang by my knees and swing. I'd turn upright by gripping the bar with my hands and then flipping my legs over my head so that I somersaulted to the ground, landing on my feet. It was the only trick I knew, and I did it over and over.

Lying on the table, I recalled the sensation of being upside down, of gripping the bar, of flipping my legs, ready to bring them over. And then I felt my left hand give, saw the ground rushing up, felt the back of my head striking the earth. My ear and neck ached. Feet rushed toward me—my mom's.

I'd ended up with a concussion.

And apparently my shoulder still felt guilty.

On the surface, this sounded far-fetched. But the faint scent of vanilla wafted from the massage therapist's hands, the candlelight danced on my eyelids, my body had softened, and my mind was drifting. Instead of spiraling into thoughts of disbelief, I cataloged the things I'd learned to feel in my body over the last year:

- joy: an expansion in my chest, like a rose opening to the sunset sky
- lies (both mine and other people's): a tightening in my throat, thick and gluey
- a pending fight: an itch in my nose, usually just one nostril
- creativity stymied: a pinch in my ovary
- being untrue to myself: a crack in my left ankle. If I ignored it, my ankle would refuse to support me. It won't be true if I won't.

I had learned that emotions lived in every part of me.

Apparently, memory did too.

My left shoulder remembers dropping me and feels guilty about it. Suddenly, I found I could make that leap.

32

To understand how another feels—in their body, in their soul—be their mirror. Set your intention to feel what they feel, then mimic the way they stand, the way they sit, the way they cock their head. Find their favorite turn of phrase and roll it off your own tongue. As you do, tune in to your body and see what seems different; watch your thoughts and see what flits across your mind.

The phone shrilled into the silence of a surprisingly warm winter afternoon. The ground had thawed, mud-scenting the air; the sun was a smile, a benefi-cence, reflecting off the siding and heating the worn floorboards of the porch. I smiled back from within my blanket cocoon. I was sitting in my new-to-me porch rocker, using my foot to send the chair back and forth, back and forth. The rocker was part of a late-night purchase from the local auction house: I'd bought a pair; both were wicker but one was a blue-gray and the other a dusky green. Everyone else at the auction seemed to have forgotten that summer would come again, but I could already feel the shift: energy rising after autumn's long descent. The rockers had been placed on the stage, the lot number read, and the brief description: *pair of rockers, good condition.* Bidding started and I had the adrenaline rush of raising my paddle. I could see the chairs clearly on the wraparound porch; I knew they were mine. There wasn't even a fight. I held my breath as the auctioneer said, "GOing ONCE! GOing TWICE..." He seemed to find fresh energy as the evening wrapped up, the final sales announced with extra vigor. I had begun to suspect he was trying to keep himself awake.

I'd become a Wednesday night regular at the auction. Two hilarious older women, bedecked in fuchsia lipstick and bedazzled baseball caps, always set up a folding table near the door where they sold smoked kielbasa topped with surprisingly tasty sauerkraut. The first time they remembered my name was a little thrill. I was a Beaconite! Beth from the antiques store was often there, and the woman who'd opened a boutique on Main Street made an occasional appearance. Jim, whom I'd met through Beth, had an engineering gig on Broadway by day but did professional-level antique restoration for relaxation; he was often there, too, and could be counted on to help me get my stash home. He'd dropped off the rockers earlier, and while he was at the house, I got him to adjust the front doors, which were sticking.

The phone handset was propped on the windowsill where it could still connect to the wireless receiver inside. The sash was open just a smidge and John Hiatt's voice drifted through the crack. I'd had the CD on repeat since lunch:

I'll be there, I'll be there to catch your fall
So have a little faith in me. . . .

The phone rang again, less startling this time but still loud. I scrambled to answer it.

"Hey, Mom. What's up?" I asked, seeing her name on the caller ID. We spoke Sunday mornings. An off-schedule call was often for something specific.

"Shingles, unfortunately. I know you've never had it, but I'm wondering what you might do if you did?" She knew I'd been experimenting with herbal remedies. "Is there anything that can help?"

Umm, wow. I rocked a few times, a little stunned. Mom was asking me to help. Mom *trusted* me to help. Huh.

"Oh wow, Mom. I'm sorry. That sounds awful." And it did. I'd seen photos of the lesions and heard people talk about how intensely painful shingles could be. "How 'bout I do a little research and call you back?"

After we hung up, I gathered the blanket and phone and went inside. My herbal library had grown, but I still reached for *Prescriptions* first. It had good descriptions of different ailments, and beyond the photos I'd seen and what people had said about their own experience, I didn't know much about shingles. Pulling it and a few herb books off the shelf, I headed for the sofa.

After forty minutes of reading, I had a list of possibilities. What I didn't have was a way to narrow them down. Mom wasn't going to try eight different things. It would be a miracle if she'd do two. I tapped the pen against my lower lip in time with the music. She'd probably be leery of taking anything internally that was unfamiliar. Plus, the doctor had put her on Valtrex already, so she didn't need an antiviral. I crossed lemon balm and Saint-John's-wort tinctures off the list. So maybe a topical? Or a supplement she'd recognize and feel comfortable with? I thought back through the conversation. She'd asked if there was anything for the burning. So a topical for pain. And maybe a supplement, something familiar, like vitamin A or fish oil.

Going back through my notes, that still left a lot of choices. Mom needed an easy, clear plan. I didn't feel like I was skilled enough to choose for her; I was still a beginner myself. Pursing my lips, I tapped the pen against them. *Tap, ta-tap, ta-tap.* If it were for me, I would choose by doing the body pendulum I'd learned from Barbara Hall. I used it so often now, it was almost second nature. I'd even figured out that I could write the name of a plant on a piece of paper and use that instead of a jar of herbs. It saved time and money, allowing me to buy only what I needed.

Tap, tap, tap went the pen.

And then I had a thought: *could I pendulum for my mom?*

Excited, I ripped a piece of paper from the notepad and tore it into strips. Each choice got its own length of paper. Carefully, I folded them into little squares, cupping them all in my hand so I could shake them around. Then I tilted them onto the coffee table and moved into the open space in front of the TV. Over the months, I'd developed a routine around penduluming. First, I shook out my arms, bounced on my toes, and rolled my neck, feeling into my body. After taking a few deep breaths, I cataloged how I felt, noting anything achy or unusual. Next, I got myself grounded, imagining my feet growing roots to anchor me. Then I stretched my "branches" skyward, extending my body, imagining myself as a line of energy between earth and sky. I set an intention, not for myself this time, but for my mom:

that I would feel a connection through those little squares of paper—to the things that would be most helpful and healing.

When I felt ready, I went into the kitchen and pulled my own supplements and herbs, the ones I was currently taking, from their shelf next to the coffee mugs. One at a time I ran each one through my chakras, asking, *does Mom need this?* I already knew I did. But I had to establish if I could pendulum for someone else. If I got all *yeses,* then it would be pretty obvious I was just penduluming for myself. But the motherwort was an immediate no. So was the evening primrose and the vitex. I could do this!

Swinging my hips and dancing a little as John sang: *We were always looking for true north. With our heads in the clouds, just a little off course . . .*

I returned to the living room. Standing in front of the coffee table, I reached for a random paper square. Holding it over my head, between my palms, hands in prayer position, I set a more specific intention: *Let me find the two best things for Mom's shingle pain.* After that it was easy: one at a time, I tested the squares of paper, grinning and bopping, making a "yes" pile and a "no" pile.

I laughed out loud when I finished the testing: there were two paper squares in the "yes" pile.

33

You can't open up the light quickly; people get blinded. You have to just hint at something—awakening them, not alarming them.

—Llorraine Neithardt, *New York Times Magazine,* November 5, 2000

The tape recorder clicked closed; a new cassette was ensconced within.

"I'll tape our session so you'll have it for reference." Llorraine's voice was raspy and rich. "Sometimes on a second listen you'll catch things you missed."

She looked, with her dark auburn hair piled in a messy knot on her head, more like a Hollywood starlet than a psychic. *You have no idea what a psychic looks like,* I reminded myself. I'd never been to a psychic. But she was one of Gail's teachers, and I trusted Gail. Plus, the stodgy professor who roamed the halls of my psyche was intrigued by her wide-ranging studies: Jungian psychology, Hermetics, Kabbalah, mythology, and symbolism. But what ultimately compelled me to fund an appointment (which seemed more like an extravagant lark than a necessity) was Gail intoning *it's time for you to see Llorraine.* Like seeing Llorraine was an initiation, the next necessary step in the Hero's Journey of my life. A shimmy of pride-laced trepidation squiggled through my gut.

"If you hear the recorder stop, remind me to flip the tape; sometimes I get going and don't hear it." Llorraine laughed hoarsely and reached for the porcelain teacup at her elbow.

"Any questions before we begin?" She had set the teacup down, and one hand hovered over the record button as she reached for her cards with the other.

I had so many questions, but most of them were along the lines of *how did you think to pair a leopard print rug with formal furniture?* Her uptown apartment was eclectic and elegant, nothing like I expected. My best city bag looked rather frumpy squatting on a cheetah-spotted pouf. Somehow the cheetah spots came off as sleek, harmonizing with the antique furniture and not clashing with the rug. Quality antique furniture, I should add. The cream upholstery was perfect, barely kin to the shabby chic pieces that adorned the Beacon blue house.

I was busy picturing Llorraine in a chignon and Chanel suit when she raised an eyebrow. Flushing, I returned my eyes to the gold-and-glass coffee table where the deck waited. "No questions," I murmured.

Instead of laying a spread, Lorraine flipped a card. As she studied it, something within her ignited, the tape recorder clicked on, and the session began. I'd decided on the train, listening to the *clack, clack, clack* of the wheels and watching the snake of the Hudson slide by, that I wouldn't tell her anything, just listen to see what she knew. But sitting in the time-slip that was her living room, where seventies chic danced with Edwardian charm, I quickly realized that wasn't the way it worked. The oracle opened to the question, responded to the emotion, was triggered by a bit of personal history. Llorraine slid effortlessly back and forth along my timeline, opening doors and windows, peeling back the rugs and peering underneath. The cards flipped, sometimes fast, sometimes slow. They too were triggers, switch points changing the track of the conversation. She wasn't laying a spread for me, instead she was using the tarot the way a mushroom hunter uses a truffle pig, letting each flip unearth a dirt-covered secret.

"The muses have had it with your temper tantrums," she reported crisply, staring at the cards. She had just informed me that my inner five-year-old was indulging in self-righteous rage because other people couldn't see her soul. This was obviously not a *you're going to marry a handsome man and have three children* kind of reading. "Honor the five-year-old by growing up. There's work to be done," she chastised me. "And, honey, do what you're supposed to do this time around. Earth is not your favorite planet."

But what was I supposed to do? I'm ashamed to admit this, but I whined and wheedled. There was a mortgage to pay; I had responsibilities—to the farm school, to Quinn and Annette. Also, I truly didn't feel like I had a calling or greater life's purpose, much as I desperately wanted one.

"But I don't know what this work is that I'm supposed to be doing! I keep trying things, and they don't stick! I was thinking about going back to school." My voice gained strength as I warmed to my topic. "Maybe getting my PhD in religion. I've read about Buddhist monks who . . ."

Llorraine flipped a card. "You're not a Buddhist monk. When you get up there," she pointed straight up, "and report to the divine, what are you going to say? *I saw nothing and did nothing during my time on Earth. I spent my time in meditation so I could be here with you?* Karma's gonna kick your ass back down here and tell you to use your eyes and ears this time! Honey, you aren't meant to be a Buddhist monk." She took a sip of tea. "Or to write a bunch of academic papers about Buddhist monks."

"Maybe I just need a sign," I offered.

That was rewarded with another throaty chuckle. "The last thing you need is a sign. You ask for a sign, then you ignore it, so you ask again. Then you ignore it again. The whole thing escalates, and all of a sudden, your rainstorm is a tsunami. *You* especially should not be asking for signs. You want a sign?" She flipped a card. "The labyrinth is your next sign."

"But . . ."

"If you were some schlubby young soul, I might accept this whinging. But you? You are a kick-ass magician and you've been manifesting for a hell of a long time. From you, this all sounds"—she made a *pffft* sound. "A wisewoman shouldn't go around saying"—she mimicked a child's petulance—"'but what about the mortgage?'" She flipped a card, then another. "Start saying *yes* to destiny."

I'd never liked saying "yes" to higher powers, so I quipped, "What a big word, *yes.*"

She smiled knowingly. "You can drown before you come to the end of it."

"I may need to say no a few more times. Scream it. Get it out of my system." I was bargaining, and she took it seriously.

Considering me, she flipped another card and studied it. "This might help. Stamp your right foot and say *I have learned all I need to from* _____." She paused, looking up. "Here you insert whatever you need to move on from. It can be anything. You might have a long list," she said dryly, reaching for her teacup. After a sip she added, "You're just a little stuck in the mud, dear. You'll get out."

34

When you walk between the worlds, visiting the inner realms, imagine opening a door on the way in. On the way out, go through the same door, closing it firmly behind you. This will train your brain to only journey intentionally to that place where everything is archetype and metaphor.

"Em, are you wearing new pants?"

"Nope," I said cheerfully. "And good morning." I smiled at Thomas, not sure how he'd gotten in. School officially started in five minutes. In the morning, adults were stationed at the goat pen and the garden, where the chickens would be loose. The kids could visit the animals or wait in the lobby, giving the teachers some quiet time to get organized. I was sitting at my classroom desk. It was two days since my meeting with Llorraine. Spending Saturday in the city had set me back on lesson planning, so I was editing my notes for the day.

Thomas cocked his head to one side, then the other, shrugging unconsciously at his backpack. Seeming to suddenly realize it was still on, he turned to stow it on the row of coat hooks that took up the entirety of the wall opposite the window. Now unburdened, he sauntered closer to give me a very serious once-over while bouncing on his toes.

"A new sweater?" he tried.

I looked at the sweater my mom had knit a few years back. It was cream-colored bouclé, which I loved because even a coffee spill just beaded on the wool.

"Nope," I answered, wondering where this was going.

"Did you get your hair cut?" he asked.

I laughed. "No, Thomas. No big changes since Friday."

Undeterred, Thomas declared decidedly, "Well, you look shiny!"

Huh, I thought, considering him. *Now isn't that interesting.*

That night I went to yoga. I'd become friends with one of the teachers, which, it turned out, was a great incentive to get me to class. My yoga practice started as I drove the tree-lined road to the studio. My breathing would slow and even out as the scent of pine wafted through Rosie's cracked open windows. By the time I parked and padded inside, I had put the ongoing concerns about my students to rest. People filtered in, found their spots, began to stretch. I smiled at my friend Kate as she paced the wood floors, murmuring hellos, then I lay back to stare at the white vaulted ceiling.

At 5:30 Kate locked the door and threaded her way to the front of the room, where she'd set up a makeshift altar. Low tonal music came from the boom box that sat next to her stenciled mat. She lit an incense cone, instructing us first to sit cross-legged and then focus on our breath.

"Close your eyes and breathe," Kate said, taking a deep and audible breath herself. "That's right," she intoned as we all inhaled and exhaled. I heard her soft footsteps as she walked through the room, balancing the energy of the space, using her breath to remind us of our own.

"Before we begin, take a few moments to check in with yourself. Scan your body. . . . Just noticing, not judging. . . ." Her feet whispered across the floor as she came closer to where I was sitting. "When you're ready, set an intention for your practice this evening."

My intention came in a flash: *I intend to use this practice to feel all my past lives on a cellular level.*

To be clear: This was *not* a wisely thought-out intention. Since the meeting with Llorraine, I'd been chewing on the phrase *old soul,* which Llorraine had used multiple times. Was there really such a thing as an "old soul"? Didn't everyone think they were an old soul? Did Llorraine ever tell someone they were a *young* soul? The whole thing sounded like bunk to me.

My intention basically amounted to *Prove it!*

I was baiting the universe. (Apparently, I'd completely forgotten Llorraine's warnings about asking for signs.)

As we moved into sun salutations, stretching up and folding over, I saw cliffs, heard waves crashing, felt the layered vibrations of many voices chanting. It was soothing, expanding. But, hinging up into downward dog for the third time, something different began to happen. I felt disjointed, made from unmatched parts. The feeling continued as I tried to flow through my practice. By the time we came to dandasana, the seated staff pose, I was disoriented. Keeping my eyes closed, I focused on my breath, on using it to find my equilibrium. Suddenly my inner vision shifted, swinging like a censer. I was peering down into the dark gash of a chasm. I was not a body but a point of view, hanging over the void. An electric current flashed up through me, traveling the pathways of my spine. It was immense, consuming, untamable. I felt my limbs shaking, as though their movement could pull me back into the *me* that had a body.

The chasm. It was the chasm that made me think of Delphi. *The oracles were not wisewomen: they were burnt-out husks that power churned through, using them simply as a voice.* A fear began to rise within me. Was I being asked to give up my mind, to become a husk, a shell for something greater than me? Did the universe want me emptied out, made into a vessel? The power that was demanding to live in me was immense, and I just wanted to cry and be small. Far, far away, I could hear the gentle shufflings of the class. We shifted to savasana, lying on the floor, eyes closed. But there was nothing corpse-like about the energy that swept through me yet again, starting at the base of my spine and wildfiring upward. Heat wicked from my third eye. There was pressure in my head, and I was suddenly so very, very tired.

And then Kate was there, her hands solid and real as she gently dabbed a cooling drop of lavender on my forehead. She pushed my shoulders downward toward the mat, and I tried to use the force to send all that extra energy into the earth.

At the close of class, I struggled to sit up, to join the chanting of *Om* that ended our practice. In my mind, I once again heard voices singing. A roomful of voices, their harmonies cool on my hot limbs. Again, the ocean shushed behind my eyelids. While people said goodbye and the room cleared out, I sat and listened to the sounds reverberating through my head.

Then Kate was crouching beside me, oblivious to my inner turmoil.

"Give me a ride?" she asked. "Stephen dropped me off."

Fishing in my bag, I handed her my keys.

In the morning, my head was still buzzing. The slanting sunlight made dust motes that turned the air into a miniature field of shooting stars. That was pretty much how my insides felt, too, the remains of last night's power surge floating and drifting and pinging about.

My cards were on the bedside table. It was a new deck Quinn had bought me after hearing the common superstition that tarot cards were supposed to be a gift. Shuffling with my eyes closed, I focused on gaining advice to guide my day. When my hands stilled, one card fell onto the bedspread.

Strength.

Back on my twenty-ninth birthday, I had pulled this card. In that deck, the woman had seemed to be merging with the lion. In this deck, the lion's open maw seemed to drip with hungry saliva.

Well, that didn't bode well.

By the end of the day, I knew the Strength card intimately. Strength, I figured out, is not about the external struggles; it's about the internal ones, about coming to grips with the primal self.

My mind gnawed on the previous night's yoga class. Maybe Strength was a reminder to stay centered and grounded, true to my personal gifts; to contain myself and manage my own energy . . . which was still roaring like a riptide.

Over dinner, Annette was practical.

"Maybe you have to get this experience, this sense of free-floating energy, out of you." She thought for a moment, her spoon poised. "Sculpting doesn't feel right," she said. I'd been sculpting with self-drying clay. "Maybe a collage? Maybe you can write about it?"

This was an interesting twist. This new sense—this intuition—I'd been developing was often overwhelming. Compelling and fascinating—but also just too much. So we experimented, Annette, Quinn, and I. As I look back, it's amazing how they midwifed me through this experience, which was foreign to both of them. They took my spiritual conundrums as seriously as I took their career decisions and boyfriend woes. Whenever I got stuck, either Annette or Quinn would help me find a new way of thinking or an internal door that could be opened. We'd explored many things over the months since 9/11: ritual, exercise, breathing techniques, hot baths. Art wasn't something we'd tried before.

I thought of the windswept poems of William Blake, the angry beat of Ani DiFranco's lyrics.

Words. Words felt right. They had the power to release.

When we finished eating, I carried our bowls to the sink. Annette gently hip checked me as she brought the cutting board over to be cleaned.

"Go take a bath," she suggested. "You're in the middle of a breakthrough." When I hesitated, she gave me a nudge. "Go on; I've got this."

But I was too antsy for a bath. Instead, I curled in a rattan chair I'd found out on the sidewalk on garbage day back when I lived in Brooklyn. With a notebook balanced on the wide arm, it made the perfect writing desk. An hour later, my hand was cramped and my mind empty. I handed the loose sheets to Annette. The strokes of ink seemed to direct the energy that had been gathering within me; the edge of the page contained the flow.

Annette stood reading, a coffee mug in one hand, my pages in the other. Then she sat down hard on the cranberry velvet sofa, her head bowed over the writing still in her hand.

"This is it, Em," she said softly, reading even as she spoke. "You have to write."

35

The Roman god of transitions, Janus, rules the midpoint between the abstract and the concrete. It is a place we cross through when we're creating: taking an idea and giving it material form. It is also a place we move through when we are unwinding, allowing something concrete to return to formlessness.

That weekend I visited the old Methodist cemetery. It was an odd place, marooned without a church in one of Beacon's northern neighborhoods. Despite being surrounded by homes, it had an abandoned feel, the gravestones topsy-turvy—some lying flat, others listing at precarious angles. Most of the headstones were from the 1800s, their dates fading into the limestone and rimmed with moss, names receding beyond recognition. This was where I went when I needed to lay my internal agitations to rest.

On the way in, I wound through the oldest stones, the nameless ones, to visit Caroline, great-great-granddaughter of our second president, John Adams. Her name was long gone from her cracked marble headstone, but a small plaque had been added next to the grave to memorialize her. I'd found both the grave and the plaque when I first stumbled upon the cemetery.

"Hi, Caroline," I whispered, crouching to run my fingers over the marble of her headstone, caressing the place where perhaps her name had been. Reaching into my pocket, I pulled out a small rock, egg-smooth, which I'd found in the front garden under Quinn's Russian sage.

It's a Jewish custom to leave a stone when visiting a burial site. As I rolled the rock between my fingers, I pondered the relationship between stones and death. . . . the Earth element. Perhaps this tradition is a way of saying *I honor you as your body goes back to earth.*

When my knees began to ache from squatting, I touched the marble one last time, feeling the moss and lichen under my fingertips as I said goodbye. While I always stopped to visit Caroline, my true destination was the patch of green between three twisty trees that hunched in the far corner. Something about the way the gnarled roots tangled with the fallen headstones felt ancient to me, older than the town itself or the bodies buried here.

Tomorrow the moon would be full and tonight promised to be bright and clear. As the winter sun flamed out, the moon waited in the wings, bursting and ripe. I spindled between the sun to the west and moon to the east, swinging my arms loosely about my waist as I twisted, ending to beginning, sunlight to moonlight. The old trees glowed silver to welcome the coming dark.

"Goodbye, sun," I whispered to the setting orb as I stood in the center of the tiny maple grove. "Hello, moon." I swung my arms, rotating between them: sun, moon, sun, moon. My twisting became a small circle, moving counterclockwise, east to north, north to west. As I walked, I called to the moon to stand witness, my voice gaining strength, a sense of separation from the world unspooling from my heart.

"Help me release what I don't need to carry," I murmured, looking at the moon and thinking of aspects of my life that constantly gnawed at me: the struggle to find the right work, the sense of not having a purpose, the lack of partnership. I pulled out the incense and lighter I'd tucked into my coat's big pocket. As I continued to walk, I lit the incense: the earthy scent of vetiver wafted upward. My feet kept moving, scribing their tiny circle. "Help me release what I don't need to carry," I repeated, this time thinking about my money worries, how I barely scraped by even with two housemates. The incense billowed skyward. *Release all that energy with the smoke,* I coached myself, before saying the words a third and final time: "Help me release what I don't need to carry!"

And then I stopped.

My throat felt like it was still vibrating, even though the words were gone. I took a breath, inhaling deeply. My lungs expanded and expanded, like they could suddenly hold more air. The moon was higher in the sky, but it was still not fully dark.

Remembering Llorraine's suggestion, I stamped my foot once, feeling a little foolish. I looked around. Only the maples were watching, rustling their leaves as if to say *get on with it!* So I stamped my foot again, letting go from the deep places of my body—from my sinews, my cells—all I had released. With the final stamp, I asked the graveyard's dead to accept the parts of me that were ready to be laid to rest.

The incense had burned down. I wet my finger and thumb with my tongue and pinched out the last of the flame. As I stuck the stick into the ground, burnt end down, I let the last of the otherness, the timelessness of my small circle, waft from me. Instead I focused on the present: the distant rumbling of traffic on the interstate, the woodsy scent of the cemetery's spruce trees, the faint buzz from the streetlights as they blinked on.

The sun was gone from the sky. Jan and the light bulb notwithstanding, I'd never been enthused about ghosts. I certainly didn't want to run into one on a near-full-moon night in the cemetery. The thought tightened my chest and I shivered. It was time to head home.

As I turned toward the street, I remembered something else Llorraine had said: I get to choose my experience of the unseen world.

I paused at the edge of the grass, about to step onto the sidewalk. *I get to choose my experience of the unseen world.* Feeling safe with the streetlights at my back, I turned and faced the graveyard.

"Okay," I said to the empty air. "I don't know what happens when we die. I can't imagine you're all just hanging out here, but if anyone's around, spread the word: I don't want to see ghosts. That's not how I want to experience the energy of death." I paused, listening. A truck chuffed in the distance, but otherwise it was quiet. "Thanks," I added, just to be safe.

As I was walking the final blocks to my house, it occurred to me: I probably didn't need to let the ghosts know my boundaries; it was simply a matter of setting them for myself.

Something in me shifted after my visit with Llorraine. She modeled how to live in two worlds at once: She was a sharp (and fashionable!) business-woman and, simultaneously, she walked through the energetic planes gathering information, trusting her senses to guide her. There was no dichotomy: Her metaphysical work supported her physical life. Cultivating her intuition hadn't made her into a husked-out oracle, a pseudo-reality junkie, or any of the other worst-case scenarios I'd imagined for myself. Llorraine had integrated her inner world with the outer world. She was whole.

While still wobbly, I suddenly felt I had the skills to both pedal and steer the metaphoric bike I'd been learning to ride. My intuition and inner senses were part of *me,* not some exterior boogeyman. And once I stopped spinning and questioning, what I could sense in the energetic undercurrents was startling and beautiful: the pull of the moon, the swelling of the coming spring, the quickening of the witch hazel tree in the side yard . . . my place on the web.

Llorraine's no-nonsense approach stopped my tailspin. Her demand that I do something useful with my skills created a sense of normalcy:

You're good at cooking? Become a chef.

You're good with your intuition? Become a _____?

That was still the question.

Coda

A journal entry, January 25, 2002

Naming has been a powerful symbol in my life. I think all the screwing around with my name has been a search for my true name: my purpose for this life. To be named truly is to be called . . . and thus the hero's quest begins.

The Road to Ireland

2002–2003

To walk a sacred path is to discover our inner sacred space:
that core of feeling that is waiting to have life breathed back
into it through symbols, archetypal forms like the labyrinth,
rituals, stories, and myths.

—Lauren Artress, *Walking a Sacred Path*

36

In Jewish mysticism, eighteen represents the word חי or life. Thirty-six is two eighteens, therefore two lives. The goal, then, is to balance and bridge these two lives: the exterior life and the interior life. When you can do that, you've discovered magic.

A vine had volunteered in the compost heap. A seed, scraped from a gourd for some long-ago meal and now burrowed deep in the pile, tested the spring air and sent forth a cotyledon. We didn't notice it then. It was tiny and we were busy. Quinn was spending more nights at her boyfriend's, and Annette was often in the city. Following the tugs of intuition, I'd signed up for a writing conference, had taken a weekend labyrinth workshop, and spent twelve days traveling in Asia with my aunt and uncle. All these adventures should have been impossible on my teacher's salary, but as each opportunity arose, a way to pay would become apparent: a house-sitting gig, a weekend job, a gift from my parents. Something had shifted for me after Llorraine, after the realization that I had tools to channel energetic overflow. Knowing I could craft my experience of the inner worlds in much the same way my mom used to encourage me to reframe my dreams allowed me to stretch and experiment. When I described the change to a friend, she said, "Oh! It's like when Luke got a light saber. At first, he's whipping it around, acting like a punk, just kind of fascinated with his special toy. But then he realizes he needs to practice so he can actually do something with it; that it's more than just a cool thing to play with." In the spring of 2002, I turned my energy toward constructively channeling my inner senses toward useful outward endeavors.

At the same time, unbeknownst to any of us, the cotyledon in the compost heap grew and grew. By the end of spring, it had curled through the backyard. We were charmed when we noticed it in early summer, adorned with marigold-hued blooms. A few weeks after that, tiny gourds speckled the vine. To add to the bounty, the mulberry trees were surprisingly prolific that year. In late August, I hauled a ladder from the garage so I could climb its aluminum treads, a basket on my arm, to reach the higher branches. One basket filled, then the next. Mulberries can be seedy and tart, but that summer they were sweet. I made pies for weeks. Friends learned of the baking spree and stopped by after work or on their way home from the weekend flea markets. The house seemed content, full of visitors and the wafting scent of warm sugar. In September, the Wednesday night auction yielded two antique scythes, which I thought to use instead of the lawn mower. That was a fail. *Buffy the Vampire Slayer* began its final season. I'd gotten Annette, Quinn, and a few other friends addicted, so on Tuesday evenings we gathered in front of the TV. Knowing the end was near bonded us; it was rare for anyone to miss an episode. In this way, spring became summer and then summer gave way to autumn.

One night after dinner, Annette, Quinn, and I bundled on jackets and took our mugs to the front porch. Halloween had come and gone. We had tried to carve the gourds from the volunteer vine but found they were much too small for carving. Quinn had instead brought home a big round pumpkin, which now sported a collapsing, gap-toothed grin. It, too, would soon end up on the compost heap.

The days were noticeably shorter. The sun had dipped westward into the river while we were inside eating and the sky was darkening to indigo. Overhead, two V's of late geese winged past, one after the other. I couldn't make out the details of their underbellies in the fading light—they were simply silhouettes heading south. A poem I'd taught my second graders at the Illustrious Private School drifted through my mind as I leaned my head back to watch them: "Something Told the Wild Geese." It was about how the geese knew when to leave, when to head to warmer climes. Annette sat one step up from me, her shearling-slippered foot next to my hip. Quinn had seen a weed she couldn't let live and, after pulling it, had stretched out in the garden, despite the cold. Her upper body was half under the skeletal remains of the Russian sage, her legs crossed on the path's pavers. Tilting my head to the side, I butted Annette's knee. She mussed my hair, distracted. I took a sip of tea, the cup's rim warm against my lips. Putting it down, I bumped her, again, gently.

"What's up?" I asked. "You're pensive."

Quinn stopped staring at the underside of the sage and rolled to face us. Annette cradled her thick pottery mug, staring into it as though she could read the tea leaves through the liquid. A car *vroom*ed, shifting gears in the distance.

"I'm moving back to Manhattan," Annette finally said. Her voice was softer than usual. "In January or February. I thought I'd build a life here but . . . " She shrugged, shaking her head. She'd tried, unsuccessfully, to get a job in Beacon.

I wanted to protest. Just last month, she'd been talking about buying a giant Quan Yin carving for the garden. That didn't seem like something you did if you were planning to leave. We'd visited a Buddhist monastery in Carmel. Annette had been enthralled by a Quan Yin statue there; she'd said it emanated peace. The visit had followed a series of conversations about the nature of God. During one of those discussions, Quinn had commented, "I finally realized that God doesn't have time for chitchat. You just have to take a number and sit really still." This led to speculation about meditation, which Annette and I followed up with a trip to the Buddhist monastery. The teaching that day was about clinging. Clinging can be directed at anything, the monk told us: an object, an idea, a word, a person.

I wanted to cling; I couldn't imagine the house without Annette. Instead, I stayed silent and breathed and felt. In that stillness, I could almost see the silken strand spooling from her, a tightrope back to New York City. Her life was still there. She'd never really taken root in Beacon. She always looked slightly out of place, like Sophia Loren visiting the small-town cousins.

My tea was turning tepid in the cool night air. I sipped anyway, giving myself another minute. Quinn hummed under her breath, her way of taking a pause. One star appeared in the sky, then another. At overnight camp I'd learned the names of the constellations, but never the individual stars.

At other points in my life, I might have tried to change her mind. But much as it ached to admit it, Annette was right. I could *feel* the rightness, as if a puzzle piece suddenly clicked in somewhere unexpected and, when it did, it became obvious why it hadn't fit in other places. So I said nothing. Just sipped my cooling tea and leaned my head against her knee. My eyes filled with tears. I didn't want Annette to feel bad, seeing me cry, but I trusted the darkness to keep my secret.

Sometimes I wonder what would have happened if she'd stayed. The year before I'd bought the blue Victorian, the DIA Art Foundation had purchased the old Nabisco plant down by the train station. It was going to be renovated to house the foundation's oversized sculpture collection. For my first couple years in town, no renovations seemed to be happening; the factory looked as abandoned and decrepit as ever. But then came a flurry of activity. Windows were replaced and hardscape installed. The town was changing too. It was subtle. The boarded-up end of Main Street, the end closest to both my house and the new museum, now sported an art gallery and a coffeehouse, lone outposts on an otherwise deserted thoroughfare. But they were harbingers of a future—one that was closer than we realized that November night on the porch. The museum was scheduled to open in May, in less than six months. On the weekends, Mercedes and Audis had begun to crawl down the streets, standing out amidst Beacon's Hondas and Toyotas. *Maybe,* thought those Manhattanites as they came to explore the town the DIA museum had chosen, *this undiscovered spot would be good for a weekend house. Real estate is still cheap.*

Maybe Annette could have gotten a job at DIA. In my mind's eye, she's dressed in her cream silk blouse, the top unbuttoned to reveal a simple gold chain. She'd have a clipboard on her arm as she chatted with the museum's director, arranging the day's tour groups. At lunchtime, she'd walk up Main Street to the new Asian fusion place that would surely open once the museum was established. On the way back to work she would grab a coffee from the café that had recently gone in, dodging the flowerpots decorating the stoop to pull open the freshly painted door.

But that night sitting on the porch steps watching the stars wink into existence overhead, we didn't know there was fresh paint and sushi in Beacon's future. And, even if we did, there was still that silver thread, shimmering like the Hudson, anchoring Annette to a city ninety minutes south.

A breeze had picked up while we were talking. I shivered, using the chill as an excuse to pull my arms in tight, hands on my cheeks to brush away the tears. Spilling the remains of my tea into the azalea at the base of the steps, I stood and offered a hand to Annette. She dusted her spotless slacks as I pulled her up; then, together, we grabbed Quinn's hands. We yanked but she was already bouncing to her feet, her cackling laugh making Annette and me grin despite ourselves.

As we headed inside, Quinn slung her arms around us both, a feat since she was the shortest by half a foot.

"Are you sure you want to go?" she quipped. "You're going to miss the final episodes of *Buffy*!"

Then the house hugged us in as we stepped into the warmth of the foyer.

It turned out Quinn was going to miss the final episode of *Buffy*, too. An unraveling had begun, and our lives in Beacon were falling away as surely as the leaves on the backyard's mulberry trees.

It started with Annette's announcement. Then, less than a week later, a call came from Patricia, the director of a youth-based not-for-profit where I had taken a part-time job to help fund my extracurricular activities. Their accountant had found an error. They'd misbalanced the books. What they had thought was *$91,000* was actually *$9,100*. My position was terminated, effective immediately. I was shocked . . . but I also, somehow, wasn't. As I hung up the phone, after assuring Patricia I was fine—shocked, but fine—something within me sensed a new pattern. It was as though I'd crested a hill and could now survey the downward slope before me; I was at the point where up becomes down. There was a loosening in my lungs. Then the seed of a thought: *If my life in Beacon was unraveling, I didn't have to cling.* I didn't have to try to piece it back together. I could walk through the gates, letting go, and letting go, and letting go. Part of my mind said, *What an odd train of thought.* But another part simply said, *Yes.*

37

The inner world is a land of metaphor and mirrors. Action reflects intention. This is the heart of a "spell." You take the metaphors of the inner world and you act them out in the outer world, thus setting an intention into motion. So, to release yourself from old commitments and thoughts that bind you, cut the cord. Snip a thread or string with scissors while intending to release what no longer serves.

And so began the unraveling. Over and over, I would get still, check in with myself, feel for the energy currents.

Release, they whispered.

Quinn heard back from a job she'd applied for over the summer. It was with a nonprofit that was exploring sustainable agricultural practices. They were planning to open a farm-to-table restaurant. Last I checked, she's still a horticulturalist there, tending the gardens and leading education programs. Accepting the job meant she, too, would be moving south.

I had moments when I considered finding new housemates, starting again. But even thinking about it was exhausting: posting flyers and inter-viewing, adjusting to different people's rhythms and energies. Plus there was something about this unwinding that felt . . . intentional. A season in my life was ending. In my mind I could hear Llorraine's voice, *Start saying yes to destiny.* And while it seemed dramatic to think that this unwinding was destiny, I did have the sense of a strong current moving through my life. Perhaps that's what destiny is: a strong current. Unlike the exhaustion I felt when I contemplated starting again in Beacon, the thought of following the current of the river within brought a calm kind of joy. I talked with Gail about it at my weekly appointment, musing on how bizarre it was to purposefully dismantle a life I'd worked so hard to create.

"What's your intuition telling you?" she queried as the lights went dim. She'd already slid in the cool needles, smoothing my meridians. The door closed quietly as she left the room. I turned inward. There was no confusion.

Let go, my inner witch instructed.

So I made a decision that my past self would have found impossible—or at least implausible: I decided to assist the unraveling that had already begun. Instead of pulling against the tide, I went with it, unspinning the web I'd woven and digesting the silken threads that bound me to my life in Beacon.

It takes three silks to anchor a web. Annette and Quinn had snipped theirs. There was only one thread remaining. With a confidence that surprised me, I put the blue house on the market.

38

Many times upon a time, there was a witch.
The witch lived on a summit peak.
The witch lived by a mirrored lake.
The witch . . .

The truth is the witch's legend had fallen to fragments. Worse yet, the Lenape story had been tangled with the tale of a certain Rip Van Winkle. So now, no one really knew where the witch lived. But bits of her story remain in the lore of the Hudson Valley, and you can find them if you care to go looking. Here are the tatters I could reweave:

Many times upon a time, there was witch.

A weaver of winds and spinner of clouds, the witch lived where snowmelt streams fed a mirrored lake. Sometimes humans came to call. If they carried ripe gourds, she would shed her bobcat skin to greet them at the water's edge.

Laying her lips against the gourds' pebbled skin, she'd blow them hollow. The gourd, now a flask, was filled with fresh water. And then she would sing. She would sing to the spirit of the spring, to the essence of the creek, to the soul of the stream. Between her hands, the flask would become a womb and, inside, a river would begin to flow, a new world emerging.

Some say this is the end of the story, but I suspect it is only the beginning.

39

To calm your sympathetic nervous system, breathe in a square: in through your nose for a count of five. Hold for a count of five. Breathe out through your nose for a count of five. Hold for a count of five. Repeat as needed.

She came in a dream. It was after I'd put the house on the market but before I'd decided where I would go or what I would do next.

The real estate agent had shocked me when she suggested a listing price. It was more than three times what I'd paid.

"People are coming from Manhattan," she told me. "DIA will be opening soon."

The profit I'd make was almost inconceivable. After I paid off the mortgage, I'd have over 140,000 dollars in the bank. I decided to take a sabbatical, a full year off. But what I would do during that year and where I would live after I sold the house were still question marks. My future was an amorphous fog that was rolling closer and closer. I was in a boat, getting carried down a river. While I didn't know where the river went, riding the current was easier than hacking my way along the banks.

And then there was the dream.

It was one of the rare ones that feels real, rather than the subconscious composting that happens most nights. In my mind, the dream woman was the Catskill Witch, the Lenape woman who has whispered to the Hudson Valley's winds for centuries. Outside the Beacon house, that same wind jiggered and moaned. Shutters creaked and a door banged downstairs. The dream fled as I startled awake. In my bed, I lay frozen, adrenaline pumping from the sudden bang. The dream was receding, its images scattered.

The comforter had slipped. Tucking it under my chin, I breathed in a square, trying to calm my skittering heart. The house creaked, complaining about the storm. Last month, on a rare night when we were all still home, a window had blown out in the attic. Quinn, Annette, and I had gone up with a flashlight, sweatshirts pulled over our pajamas, to fit the frame back in place as thirty-degree air tried to whoosh through the opening. But now the house felt snug. The bang was probably the laundry room door whisking shut; the windows in there were ill-fitting. They would need to be replaced . . . but not by me.

As I calmed, the dream crept back. I saw an androgynous woman in a simple tunic, midnight-black hair touching her knees. She flew over a vast water, and I saw through her eyes.

This is where I came for my initiation: six months on the coast, saving birds.

I saw a churning gray sea, then a rugged shoreline. The land curved in a way that made me think of islands. Of Ireland, where I'd traveled for my thirtieth birthday. My mother had come with me. She was uncertain about the trip, but Dad intervened and encouraged her. It was her first time overseas without him.

More of the dream returned to me as the house continued to moan and sigh. Amid the coastal rocks, the witch had extended her arms, fingers straight, one hand atop the other, sending energy downward. She asked me to help. The waves crashed and foamed around us as I found my footing on the tumbled stone. Mimicking her stance, I held out my arms, right hand over left, palms facing the earth. My right hand seemed to be taming a rising force, while my left created space for its sister's work. The witch and I were recalibrating *something* with our gesture and intention. She held a large area and I a small one; folds in the fabric of existence were steadied by our will.

Big changes are both good and bad, the Catskill Witch instructed. *It's hard to do workings that keep the balance and are one-hundred-percent benign. There are limited magics of this balancing kind.*

Then she asked me something strange: she asked if I'd gotten tapes and videos to bring along.

Along where? I wondered, even as I told her I preferred books. She nodded speculatively, her eyes gazing into the distance, her ears attuned to things I couldn't hear.

Go, then, she said, her focus returning to me. *Go and study the birds.*

As the dream began to fade a second time, I grabbed my notebook, scribbling as quickly as possible. The bedroom was blanketed in blackness, the page a smudge of gray, the ink invisible to my eye. The house was quiet. I was the only one home. While neither had moved out yet, both Quinn and Annette were increasingly gone. Outside the window, the moon was gestating its next cycle. For now, it was just another spec of darkness in the winter sky.

I'd been thinking about what I would do after the house sold. For weeks I'd rested in the void of not knowing, unable to see through the fog and around the labyrinthine curve to what came next. In an attempt to spark my imagination, I'd started a list of everything I'd ever been vaguely interested in but hadn't had time to pursue:

weaving

pottery

herbal medicine

archaeology

photography

landscape design

jewelry making

After the night of the dream, I scrawled the word *Ireland* next to the list, circling it a few times for good measure. The instruction to *study the birds* felt metaphoric, but Ireland had tasted real, the ocean's spray salty on my tongue.

My laptop lived in the dining room, on a long rectangle of chestnut planks I'd salvaged from the antiquated coal bin in the basement. Jim, the Broadway guy who restored antiques for fun, had magically turned the old wood into a tabletop and mounted it on a surprisingly graceful metal machine base we'd found at a flea market. The table was much too nice for the house. It made everything near it seem shabby in comparison. My iBook, however, looked very sleek sitting on top of it, like it was waiting for an *Architectural Digest* photo shoot.

Dropping my notebook on the table, I turned on the computer and waited for it to boot up. Once the screen came to life, I pulled up Alta Vista (Google was not ubiquitous yet), then took my list and, one at a time, entered each term plus Ireland.

The search engine icon whirred and spun. The results were haphazard. Amid the detritus of cyberspace one search result stood out: Airmid's Academy of Herbal Arts. I clicked to the About page. A middle-aged woman with raven hair, decked out in a cloak, sat by a stone hearth. She looked uncomfortably serious in her Renaissance Faire attire. I closed the browser tab and went back to my list.

The next day I did the same thing.

And, again, the day after.

The raven-haired woman kept appearing. Finally—on the fourth day . . . or the fifth?—I clicked through to the Programs page. There it was: a two-month, live-in herbalism course beginning in early September. My stomach clenched. I toggled between the course description, which sounded reasonable, scholarly even, and the image of the witchy woman who would be my teacher.

I can't tell you for certain whether it was that day, or the next, or the next. But before the end of April, I had applied to the program and been accepted.

40

In many Asian cultures, items of importance are given and received with both hands. This formality calls the attention of both the giver and the receiver to the transaction; it calls on them to be present in the moment. Along with the physical exchange, there is an energetic one: the giver graciously releases, the receiver willingly accepts.

Tiny dewdrops still decorated the Russian sage and echinacea in the front garden as I sat on the stoop sipping my morning coffee. The house was under contract, with the closing scheduled for the last week of May. I'd spent the week flyering the local libraries and coffee shops and had run an ad in the paper for a yard sale. While I could have put my things in storage, that didn't feel true to the unwinding. If I were going to unspin this web, I would be thorough about it.

The scent of cinnamon wafted from the mug I was cradling. I looked at the heavy clay critically. *Keep or release?* The mug had a solid handle I could slide all my fingers through, which made it easy to hold. But otherwise, it wasn't particularly special. *You're overthinking this!* I told myself. I was going through this process with each item in the house—what did I want to carry into my new life? And I *was* overthinking it, which was getting exhausting.

Putting down the mug, I stood up and stretched. Time to get moving.

Between coffee sips, I carried the accoutrements of my Beacon life out to the driveway.

I'd spent the past week researching pricing for the antiques I'd collected and fixed up over the past three years. While my restorations were nothing like Jim's, everything was in working order: drawers slid and upholstery was mended. Most things were in good, but not excellent, condition, so I priced accordingly: $330 for the walnut dresser, $110 for the nightstand, $125 each for my lovingly fixed-up porch rockers.

Before the sun had risen above the mulberry trees, my first shoppers appeared. I was arranging baskets and other knickknacks when a woman pulled up in an old Volvo, taking a minute to don a floppy sun hat before getting out of the car. She carried an oversize tote that looked mostly empty. It took her just seconds to scan the furniture offerings.

"Any smalls?" she asked. *Smalls* was flea market slang for the stuff that could fit in her tote bag.

"There are a few willow baskets over there." I pointed toward the garage. "And some McCoy and Roseville flowerpots. They have chips so I priced them accordingly," I told her.

She strode over and picked up a pot to see the price tag on the bottom. She put it down. Hands on her hips, she scanned my offerings before heading back to the Volvo, calling a thank-you over her shoulder.

A few other early shoppers stopped by: an older couple, both tan and fit; a mother with a BabyBjörn slung over her chest; a woman preceded by the waft of patchouli. The results were the same: a quick look and back to the car.

By the time my friend Bill arrived, five people had stopped by and I had sold exactly nothing.

"Hey!" he called as he walked up the street toward the house. "Got anything good?"

I met him at the sidewalk. "Apparently not," I reported, hands on my hips. "Five people have been by, but no sales."

Bill was older than I was and always looked much tidier than the guys my age, with his shirttails tucked into his well-worn jeans. As usual, he had a 35mm camera slung on a long strap across his chest.

Standing on the sidewalk, we surveyed the layout. I'd created a little tableau: the dresser had a small lamp on it and a few large pots accented one side; gardening tools were artfully arranged with an antique wheelbarrow against the side of the garage.

Bill flipped the cap off his camera. It clicked as he took a couple shots. I smiled and shook my head. It was like he understood the world better when he saw it through the camera's frame.

"Looks good," he said as he checked his shots on the LED. We'd had many discussions about cameras; how I missed actually twisting the lens rings to set the F-stop and adjust the focus. Modern cameras were a mental exercise: what is the best F-stop for this shot? But film cameras required a body feel; your hands began to know how to set up a picture, twisting faster than your conscious mind could follow. It was body knowledge; it was intuitive.

I glanced over Bill's shoulder. He held the camera so I could see the screen. "It does look good." I shrugged. "Still, no one's buying."

"It's early still," he assured me. He capped the camera and set it on the porch rail. "You dragged this stuff out by yourself?"

"Yup." I raised the coffee mug to my lips and sipped air. Chagrined, I looked into the empty mug.

"Impressive," he said. "What still needs doing?"

Walking over to the walnut nightstand (price $110), I grabbed a Sharpie and masking tape from where I'd laid them and held them out to Bill. "Can you pull things out of the garage? Nothing in there's too valuable. You can probably price most of it between $15 and $30. Except for those scythes. Those should be $75 each."

Bill raised his eyebrows.

"Okaaayy," he said, spacing out the syllables of the word as he took the pen and tape from my hand.

At the end of the day, I'd sold two things. The largest willow basket went to a woman who had driven up from New York City where, she told me, she had an antiques shop. Her companion for the day was a miniature Yorkie named Samuel. I got the dog a bowl of water; I think that's why she bought the basket.

The second item sold was an unusual and incredibly heavy square antique mirror, which hung point up. It had a six-inch-wide cherry frame. In all my time antiquing, I'd never seen another one like it. Hal admired it and insisted on paying full price: $85. Beth, who had swung by in the late morning, pretended to fight him for it.

By four o'clock it was apparent that those were going to be my only sales for the day.

The next weekend I repeated the process. But this time I realized I'd priced things too high: antiques shop prices are not yard sale rates. After arranging everything in the driveway again, I took a red pen and slashed through the original numbers, making everything half off.

It was after this second yard sale that I realized I was clinging. In my mind, I was unraveling my Beacon life, while in reality I was still grasping at it. The various artifacts of my time in the blue house—the baskets and cupboards and flowerpots—still had value to me, and I was expressing that value right on the yard sale price tags.

Quinn and Annette had both moved out. Gail had already given me a travel gift, a small statue of Quan Yin. There was only one weekend until the closing, when the blue house would become someone else's. It was time to say goodbye . . . and really mean it.

The house felt alert as I padded across the oaken floors. In the dining room, I touched the plaster walls, remembering the layers of ancient wallpaper, the gummy feeling left behind after I'd steamed them off, chunks of paper losing their grip and sliding to the floor. The plaster was cool and smelled chalky as I pressed my cheek to it. *Thank you,* I whispered. The plaster had always felt reassuring, like the soft inner lining of an egg. I stayed there a moment, memorizing the scent, then I used my fingers like invisible scissors and cut the energetic ties that bound me to the house's walls. I gave the smooth surface a pat before moving on to the industrial dining table. Laying my palms on its surface, I recalled the look of the boards when they'd come up from the basement, stained with water and coal dust but still wormy chestnut—rare since the blight. Mostly the table made me think of Jim, who'd turned out to be a good friend. When I wielded my invisible shears, I set in my mind to unbind the table, but keep the friendship.

In this fashion, I made my way around the house. *Goodbye,* I whispered to the pocket doors, sliding them open and closed. *Thanks,* I murmured to the claw-foot tub. As I processed through the rooms, I began to feel lighter, more filled with joy and less stodgy. Eventually I ended up in the front room with the bay windows. It was empty except for some boxes piled against the far wall and the sheer dotted curtains on the windows facing the street.

Pacing counterclockwise in a circle, I stopped at each of the four directions, crouching with my hands on the floor in the spots where I'd often laid out bowls of water, candles, feathers, and potted plants representing the four elements. There were no tools in my hands now, no representations linking me to the metaphoric realms; there was just me, the empty room, and the circle I could feel. Facing west, I thanked the Hudson, the water that bisected my very real landscape. Pacing south, I crouched down, the oak floor smooth against my fingertips, and thanked the sun for ripening the mulberries along the back fence line. East I thanked for the words that had flowed during my time in the blue house—for my conversations with

Annette and Quinn that had guided my way. And north held my gratitude for the land itself, which had supported all of us for a time.

———————

Morning came, cloudless and clear. It was Saturday, less than a week until closing. I sat on the porch steps as the yard-salers arrived. This was sale number three. There was a giddy feeling in my veins, rising like seltzer, glistening like soap bubbles. Once again, I'd pulled everything out to the driveway, but this time, the prices were all between one and five dollars.

"Hi," I called to a woman carrying a brightly colored market basket as she crossed from the other side of the street.

She smiled. "Are you moving?"—a conversation starter, not a real question, since the answer was obviously yes. The SOLD sign was spiked in the catmint next to the garage.

"Yup," I responded, putting down my coffee and getting to my feet. She had walked up, with no car in sight. "You local?"

"Just moved in," she said as she ran her finger over the back of one of the porch rockers. "These are nice." Gathering her skirt, she sat down in the smoke-colored one, giving a little push with her foot to start it rocking. Her fingers ran speculatively over the armrest.

"Do you have a porch?" I asked.

"Mm-hmm," she nodded. "We had it rebuilt before we moved in."

I knew the house. The porch ran along its length, punctuated by floor-to-ceiling double doors. It was unusual. Gothic feeling, but also sort of industrial.

"Sounds like you need a housewarming gift," I said. "It's a neighborhood tradition," I improvised. "When I moved in, Mrs. Cahill brought a pie. I don't have a pie but maybe these rockers?"

The woman blinked at me, obviously baffled. I sat down next to her in the other chair.

"I'm moving to Ireland. These rockers would look great on your porch. It would make me happy to know they were still in the neighborhood. . . . And

Mrs. Cahill really did bring me a pie." I smiled and indicated the house across the street with my chin.

"I..." she started, then paused. "Are you serious? It's incredibly generous."

"It would make me happy," I said, realizing as the words left my mouth that they were true.

Something shifted in her face, something that made me think that if I'd been staying, we would have become friends. "Then it would make me happy, too. I'm Stacey, by the way." I took her offered hand, feeling the sparks and bubbles leaping between us—a little bit of joy, shared.

And that's the way the day continued. If someone admired a basket or trinket, I offered it to them. Strangers protested, but then I'd explain I was about to go off on an adventure and couldn't take whatever it was—a vase, a throw pillow, a dresser—with me. That it would make me happy to know it was loved. The reciprocal joy I felt with Stacey and the rockers doubled and tripled as I giddily slashed prices and gave things away. A little boy offered me a polished stone in exchange for an iron, dog-shaped doorstop. An older woman, her lipstick candy pink, kissed my cheek when I gifted her three antique flowerpots. A neighbor from down the street teared up when I told her the walnut dresser and the matching nightstand were five dollars. She was unexpectedly supporting her two grandchildren and could use the help. Still, she would have been insulted if I'd given her furniture for free.

With each exchange the well-wishes for my Ireland trip grew. It felt like an energetic buoy lifting me high above uncertainty, making my choices seem more and more right.

As the afternoon sun crept toward the west, I was pleased to see the garage and driveway were nearly empty. I had promised the dining room table, my heavy bed frame, and the sofa to various friends. They'd be picked up the day before closing, just six sleeps away.

41

In the folklore of many cultures, names have power. In the Scandinavian lands, magical creatures can be defeated if you call them by name. In German mythology, naming a weapon increases its power and grants it something akin to a personality. And even Bilbo Baggins, the hobbit in Tolkien's Lord of the Rings books, knew better than to reveal his name to the dragon, Smaug.

"Hi, Cheryl," I greeted the receptionist, pulling the heavy door shut behind me. The air-conditioning was cranked, and she had on a light sweater.

"Paperwork's all set," she said cheerfully. "He'll be with you in just a minute."

I headed for a prim settee on the far side of the room, well away from the ice-cold window unit. Although I'd been walking by this brick-block of a building for the past three years, it was only in the last two months that I'd begun stopping in.

It had all started with a conversation over Chinese food. My class at the New Seminary, where I'd been taking courses in comparative religion, had decided to grab dinner after a Saturday lecture. Five tables were pushed together in a long snake to accommodate us. I was sitting toward one end with a few close friends. Somehow, we had gotten started on the topic of names.

"I don't know what it is with mine," I groused. "It doesn't stick. I say, *Hi, I'm Michele.* And people say, *Nice to meet you, Molly.*" Everyone was listening, so I kept going. "*I said Mi-chele. . . .* But they still don't get it! *Oh! Sorry, Melissa!* they respond."

I shrugged and speared a piece of garlicky broccoli with my chopsticks. "It's been happening for years. I have name-sheer. That's why I started going by Em."

Joanna leaned in to comment. But before she could say anything, a woman at the far end of the table, who by all rights shouldn't have been able to hear our discussion at all, yelled, "That's because your parents were supposed to name you Maia!"

The table stilled. It felt like a spotlight was shining on me. Then the strangest thing happened: everyone seemed to simultaneously sigh.

"That's it!" Francis said.

"Oh my god, it's so hard to remember *Em*," Martha admitted, reaching for the rice. "And *Michele* is worse."

I remembered my multiple birth certificates; Mom kept changing the spelling of *Michele*. First with one *L*, then two, then back again. My parents had been ready for a boy, a Michael. They scrambled when I came out female. If, as mythic stories implied, we each have a true name, what happens when you're misnamed?

"I could definitely call you Maia," Joanna said. There were murmurs of assent up and down the table.

Maia, I said to myself.

When I went home, I ran it by Annette and Quinn. This was over the winter, when both were still living at the blue house.

"I can definitely see that," Annette said.

"You'll always be Em to me," Quinn said. "But Michele is just plain bad. They obviously didn't know you." Her laugh crackled as she spooned yogurt and granola into her mouth.

In many cultures, adulthood is marked with a name change. In modern Judaism, this happens when you're bar or bat mitzvahed. But no one takes it particularly seriously, and new names are usually just the Hebrew equivalent of the name you were given at birth. But what if you took a new name and actually used it? What if you said, *I'm snipping away all the expectations of my childhood and starting fresh?* What if, instead of being given your name—your foundational signature in the universe—by your parents, you claimed the right of naming for yourself?

The idea took root. I played with spellings, *Maya, Mya, Maia.* I ran the numerology. They each had a different energy. And that made me ask: *Who did I want to be in my next incarnation of self?*

The idea snowballed. My middle and last name were soon in the mix. In the Jewish tradition, the first initial for a baby's name is taken from the name of someone who has died. I was named for my paternal grandfather, whom I'd never met. Both my first and last name honored him. My middle name was for mother's cousin Stuart, who had died in a motorcycle accident. None of the women in my lineage were represented in my naming. Nor was my step-grandpa, the only grandfather I'd ever known. A year or so before he had died, he and I were out to lunch. He'd just finished his usual turkey sandwich; a mustard smear still decorated the corner of his lip. I'd been asking him about his childhood, realizing I knew very little about who he had been. His eyes filled, which wasn't alarming—his big slobbery kisses and easy tears were part of what made him lovable. Reaching around the lunch plates, he grabbed my hands across the table. "You're my real granddaughter," he'd said, his voice thick. "I wish you had my name."

His last name was Toll. As I'd sifted through other family names, trying to figure out what went in the middle, I realized two of my great-grandmothers were named Elizabeth. If I changed the *Z* to an *S,* I could still honor my mom's cousin Stuart and my Grandma Sarah, too.

The lawyer, whose office was in a turn-of-the-century brick building near Main Street, figured out the timing so the name change would go through after the closing. There were a few unexpected steps to the process, like posting it in advance in the newspaper. A public posting felt kind of like when the officiant at a wedding asks, *Does anyone object to this union? Speak now or forever hold your peace.*

No one said "boo." Well, except my mom, but I overrode her objections.

For a few months, my attorney and I steadily worked through the name-change checklist. The last step was to send all the paperwork to the courthouse. We'd finish the paperwork and he'd deliver it after I signed the certificate of sale for the house. So a week before closing, I sat at the oval conference table in the lawyer's freezing office.

"Ready to do this?" he asked, handing me a pen.

I pulled the papers toward me. My eyes filled. Through the blur, I signed the documents that would grant me my new name: *Maia Elisabeth Toll.*

42

In the Sumerian story of Inanna, the goddess must pass through seven gates on her way to the underworld, the place of death and rebirth. At each gate, she must give up an article of clothing that represents one of her divine powers: her crown (her work and calling), her necklace (her self-expression), her beads (material security), her breastplate (her armor), her armband (her tribe and people), her rod and line (connection to inner knowing), and, finally, her robe (her human skin). It was only then that she could be reborn.

A journal entry, May 19, 2003:

I have sat calmly with this fate and railed against it, screamed why? *at the sun and the moon and the barn swallow who manages good cheer in the face of dangers I can hardly imagine. Somewhere in the depths of winter a seed was planted. Its blossom is not the expected rose but something wilder and unable to be trained.*

The stuff I've called mine is slowly disappearing: furniture, books, CDs, clothes, jewelry, the house, my name.

Who will I be without the things by which I've identified myself?

43

In a mortar and pestle, mix one part dried rosemary, one part dried marjoram, and one part dried rue. Swirl in three rose petals. Pulverize. It's okay if it's chunky. Burn to soften sadness.

Cold Spring's familiar Main Street rolled down the hill, cute shop after cute shop all the way to the river. The sun glared off the plate glass, and clumps of tourists clustered in doorways. Standing at the curb, fishing for my car keys, I felt shaky and disoriented, as if I'd been hyperventilating. It had all been so perfunctory: I signed some papers, handed over the house keys, was given a check.

"Is that it?" I asked my real estate attorney. She was my Brooklyn roommate's mom, the same person who'd sat next to me when I'd bought the house three years before.

"That's it," she confirmed before giving me a hug. "Congratulations."

I must have looked bewildered.

"I have a few more things to do here," she said. "You might want to get that check to the bank."

I crossed through the real estate agent's waiting room, leaving the cool interior behind as I opened the door. Spring was leaning toward summer. The concrete reflected the sun's heat. It was all so jarring.

Standing on the sidewalk, I took my first real breath of the day. Time, which had been behaving strangely, slowed and stretched. The sky was a robin's-egg blue with a few feathered cirrus clouds. At the end of the street, I could just make out the green-gray snake of the Hudson River. I took a few more breaths—in through the nose, out through the mouth, just like we did in yoga class. My eyes inadvertently tracked to the second-floor walk-up where Kate had moved her studio. *Goodbye, Kate!* I thought. *Goodbye, yoga class!*

A pair of women in Easter-egg colors walked by, and I stepped back toward the curb. They were laughing. Their words washed over me as sound rather than language. I could feel bands of constriction warring with the elation rising in my chest, my lungs cramping around my conflicted emotions. *Breathe,* I told myself as my new reality began to sink in: I had a very large check in my purse and was tethered to nothing. There was no mortgage to pay, no lawn to mow. I didn't have to work—for a bit anyway. There was no one to please. I was free.

I checked my phone: *1:27.* I still hadn't eaten lunch. It had been a crazy morning. The buyer had been scheduled to do a walk-through at noon, which was an hour before closing. I had thought I had everything under control. The dining room table, sofa, and bed had all been picked up the day before. With no bed, I'd slept at a hotel. It seemed tidier than sleeping at a friend's house. In the morning, I went back to the blue house to pack the last of my things into the car.

Pulling into the driveway at 9:30, I already felt like I was gone, like the house was no longer mine. But my key still slid into the lock, and my fingers did their usual quick caress of the flowers and vines on the embossed hardware. The doors swung open with ease, so different from the metal door wedged amongst the plywood that had served as an entrance when I first arrived. Now the hallway unspooled in warm woods, the vinyl and dust-colored carpet long gone. In my mind, Quinn walked by, stark naked. Sometimes she'd strip in the laundry room to wash whatever she'd been wearing. She never seemed self-conscious as she climbed the stairs to her bedroom, clad only in an empty laundry basket.

I drifted down the empty hall to the dining room, where I'd once sat on the floor trying to light candles with my mind. My fingers trailed the wall as I headed into the kitchen, Annette's domain. I could see her in her white chef's apron, her hair in a messy chignon. I could hear the precise *tap, tap, tap* of her knife on the cutting board. Light was streaming into the living room, making it look more spacious than it was.

And in the front room, the one with the bay windows . . . was a heap of stuff I hadn't been able to get rid of. Stuff I needed to sort and pack by noon.

Putting reminiscences aside, I got to work.

An hour and many trips to the car later, it became obvious the "keep" pile was significantly larger than the available space in Rosie. I tried to choose a few more things to discard, but I'd already given up so much. I'd unspooled and unwoven. I'd cheerfully ingested the silks of a web I had loved. I was exhausted. After months of carefree and efficient discarding, I'd suddenly reached my limit. I didn't want to let go of anything else. Something in me not only hit a wall but splattered against it.

What the hell was I doing? What magical thinking and crazy faith in my ability to "read the signs" had led to this ridiculous series of decisions?

My eyes stung and my throat burned. Not for the first time, the tarot's Fool flashed through my mind, whistling as he walked off the cliff. Blinking hard, I stared at the red oak floors decorated with rectangles of sunshine from the bay windows. I had adored this house since the first moment I saw it, before it was even for sale.

Trying to get myself together, I walked away from the pile of memories and out onto the porch. When I returned to the living room—ten deep breaths and a grounding exercise later—the "keep" pile hadn't gotten any smaller and my ability to deal with it hadn't gotten any bigger. I half-heartedly rearranged the mess the way you might move food around your plate when nothing is palatable.

At 11:20, I gave up and phoned Wendy. She was one of my writing friends. Something in her poet's heart had resonated with my season of releasing; we'd been meeting often to talk it through, as well as to critique each other's work. Since she was a freelance writer, I knew she'd be home midmorning on a Friday.

At 11:33, Wendy pulled up out front. Like Quinn, she was all muscle, but lithe and long, like a dancer.

"You okay?" she asked.

"I honestly don't know." I laughed. It may have been slightly hysterical. "I do know this," I said, pointing to the heap, "has to be gone fast."

She looked at the pile, then at her watch. Taking a deep breath, she said, "Okay. We can do this."

By 11:45, Wendy had ruthlessly and unemotionally sorted the remnants of my life into two piles: the one for Goodwill went into her car, and the one to keep was crammed into mine.

At 11:56, we did a quick sweep before shoving the dustpan and broom into her trunk. By noon we'd moved our cars from the driveway, parking around the corner to catch our breath. As I pulled up in front of a yellow Craftsman cottage, I realized I'd never met the neighbors who lived there. Wendy's Volkswagen chugged up behind Rosie. I got out as she walked over.

"Thank you," I said as I hugged her. She felt like a bird, light and bony. "I just . . ." I shrugged, my eyes filling with tears.

Taking me by the shoulders, she gave a little shake. "You've got this. Do you know how many people would kill to be able to do what you're doing? You're going to Ireland. To study with an herbalist." She shook my shoulders again. "Okay?" she asked, waiting for me to nod. Once I did, she surveyed my dust-covered clothes. "Come over and get cleaned up."

I looked at my watch, noticing a gritty smudge on my wrist.

"That might be good," I said, finding a smile. "But I'll only have fifteen minutes."

"Then we should get going. Michael made muffins this morning."

We climbed into our separate cars, and I drove out of Beacon.

I had made it to the real estate office with three minutes to spare. Sitting in the conference room, I'd fished in my bag for the three duplicate sets of house keys—mine, Quinn's, and Annette's. I put them on the table. My real estate agent had handed me a bottle of water and a pen. My lawyer had laid out the documents. She pointed to where I should sign. *There, and there, and there.*

The pen was surprisingly nice; the ink flowed round the smooth scrawl of my signature. I'd already begun experimenting with my new name, thinking about how I would sign future things.

Goodbye old signature.

This was surreal.

I put the pen down.

The final silk was snipped.

The remains of the web caught an updraft and floated free.

44

June 17, 2003

Re: the first step (news from the road)

Hi All!

For the past few months, I have been reading and rereading a quote from Helen Keller:

Life is either a daring adventure or nothing. Security does not exist in nature, nor do the children of men as a whole experience it. Avoiding danger is no safer in the long run than exposure.

Despite these grand and glorious words (and I am a sucker for grand and glorious words!), I must admit to a case of nerves on this day before my departure. Tomorrow, I leave for Whidbey Island, Washington, which is the first leg of this little adventure. For the next three days, I'll be driving. On Saturday, I am meeting my father in Rapid City, South Dakota. Turns out he's jealous of my newfound footloose lifestyle so he's flying to meet me for part of the trip. We will meander together from Rapid City to Billings, Montana.

I'll be spending the summer working at the Whidbey Institute and Chinook Learning Center. I have no idea what I'll be doing: I'm exchanging work for room and board. After Whidbey, I'll be going to Ireland to study herbalism. Then . . . I'll see which way the wind blows.

> Love to all,
> Maia (your friend formerly
> known as Michele!)

June 27, 2003

Re: Hello from Whidbey

Just a quick note to say I made it. The drive was alternately wonderful and grueling. Dad joined me in South Dakota and Wyoming, where we hiked in sun, rain, and snow (10″ fell in the Wyoming mountains the night before we hiked Medicine Wheel). The man sets a mean pace!

My cabin at the Whidbey Institute is a far cry from the vast spaces of the Beacon blue house. ☺ It is eight feet square, and I think the bed is what they call a *pallet*. I am, quite honestly, torn between joy at the simplicity of it all and teary because it's so overwhelmingly strange and different. But a few days of not moving at 75 mph should settle me down.

> Love,
> Maia

August 9, 2003

Re: VW vans, Vancouver, and virtuous views

Hi All!

I'm on my way to Vancouver, B.C. I've spent the last few days camping with my friend Lis's second cousin (thanks Lis!), who has a VW bus fully loaded with two beds, a refrigerator, and a stove. If you've never had the pleasure of traveling by hippie-mobile and flashing peace signs at all the other post-hippies smart enough to own one of these awesome little mobile homes, I highly recommend it. We spent three days exploring the small towns and state parks north of Seattle, hiking, beach-combing (purple starfish, who knew?), visiting friends, watching *Buffy* on DVD, building campfires, and making s'mores. It was truly wonderful.

After Vancouver, I'll be meeting my friend Joanna in Seattle. She's flying in just to hang out (yes, I feel extremely special). We have appointments with her favorite tattoo artist to expand our tats (sorry, Mom!). Once she leaves, I'll start the long haul east. It's FIVE days through the grain belt. UGH.

Hope you're all having a wonderful summer.

> With love, Mardi-gras beads,
> purple starfish, and peace signs,
> Maia

September 12, 2003

Re: Ireland bound

I'm writing on the eve of flying to Ireland. . . . This has been the "future" in my mind for quite a while. I'm ready for it to become my present.

Vancouver was pretty amazing (for the travelers: the aquarium is not to be missed). My friend Antonia took me to see an astrologer. Seems the star chart I thought was mine was 12 hours off. I feel like I've been living under the wrong stars! ☺

The drive was . . . dramatic. Three days of foul weather. The first was truly spectacular: a storm, like an ocean wave in winter, unfurling to my right, sun to my left, eighty-mile-per-hour wind gusts, tumbleweeds, and mud-buckets of rain hurling against the windshield. I kept myself calm with a recording of *The Vagina Monologues* (how panicky can you get with Eve Ensler yelling *cunt* through the car speakers?).

After that it was lots of Cracker Barrels to rent books on tape . . . More rain . . . $0.27 tea in Kansas . . . More Cracker Barrels. The odometer clocked 8,000 miles this summer. Rosie Corolla is really glad to be resting at my parents' while I'm in Ireland.

My plane leaves in a few hours. Thanks to the many friends who offered me a place to crash, a bite to eat, or a shoulder to lean on in the past few months.

Love to all,
Maia

45

Anointing is an ancient tradition meant to sanctify and make holy. Egyptian papyri contain hundreds of recipes for anointing oils. In Greek mythology, the sea nymph Thetis anointed Achilles with ambrosia to make him immortal. The Armenian Church anoints with muron, a blend of forty-eight aromas and flowers. As each new batch is produced, a few drops of the previous batch are added so that, it is said, the anointing oil always has a trace of the first batch, which was blessed by Jesus Christ.

The dining room table was strewn with notebooks and pens, bits of leaf, and piles of elderberries shining black on their fuchsia stems. The berries are medicinal and used to fight flus, but the stems are toxic and can cause nausea. The hems of our skirts were damp, the Irish mist clinging to our clothing long after we'd come indoors. We warmed our fingers on mugs of blackberry tea, letting our tongues learn the honey-sweetened taste of tannin, a class of chemical compounds that are both drying and astringent. As we waited for Eleanor's sweeping arrival, we pulled the elderberries from their stems until there were little fuchsia mounds in front of each of us and berries piling up in the bowl at the table's center.

Lucy, as usual, had three skirts layered one atop the next. On her willowy frame it was waiflike and romantic. Around the table were women who had driven in from Dublin, Navan, and Wexford. I was surprised that someone would drive so far for a three-hour class. But maybe that was because my impression of distance was based on my own interminable journey from the airport to Eleanor's house. My trip was lengthy in a way that reminded me of a movie I'd seen but can't remember the title of. The scene that comes to mind is an overflowing bus bouncing down India's roads, the driver alternately jolly and taciturn as he shouts to people along the roadside. The passengers pass food and water to each other and feed the foreigners foolish enough to have begun the sojourn without a tiffin and a few rounds of naan. On my never-ending bus trip from the airport, I had no tiffin or even a bag of Doritos. The light was soft and the air misty. The ride was a more subdued affair than the one in the movie, but still, the bus stopped six times an hour simply so the driver could crank open the door and shout a greeting to a farmer driving his sheep across the road or an older woman waiting to pick up her son (who just happened to be the cousin of the bus driver's neighbor).

Maybe I exaggerate. It's hard to say. After a sleepless night crossing the Atlantic, a connection at Heathrow, an interminable line at customs, and a two-hour wait for the bus, time was a bit of a slippery thing. Still, it took four hours for me to get from Dublin to County Westmeath, and then there was a taxi from the bus station to Eleanor's "stud." I later learned the drive was only an hour if you weren't in a bus making the magical mystery tour.

I also learned that a "stud" is a farm of sorts. It takes its name from the stallions who are kept—or in the case of my teacher's stud, *were* kept—for mating purposes. Any signs of mating had long since been erased. The stud my taxi pulled up to was now a spinster's aerie. That sounds ungenerous, but Eleanor's focus was on the plants and the rhythms of the land, not on romance, as she would earnestly tell anyone who dared to ask.

The cabdriver pulled my oversized suitcase from the trunk as I swayed on the gravel drive. Was I more hungry or tired? There was a light buzzing in my ears. Maybe that was a vote for tired. Then my eyes focused. The buzzing was the small honeybees drifting amidst the rosemary and thyme in the neatly tended gardens that bordered the whitewashed house. The driver was already carrying my suitcase up the walk when the front door opened. Eleanor stood on the threshold in a creamy white skirt with a forest green overtunic, her waist-length black hair startlingly vibrant. The driver straightened and touched his cap before turning back to me with an encouraging smile.

As the taxi turned down the drive, she ushered me in, pointing out the dining room where I was to meet her after settling into a small, simple bedroom I would share with another student—Lucy—for the next two months.

"Lucy is out for a walk. Take your time getting settled," Eleanor had said, pulling the door half shut as she left the room.

I wheeled my suitcase toward the single bed on the far wall. The one across from the door was already piled with a worn navy knapsack, a few books and a tarot deck tumbling from its unzipped top. On the nearest dresser were scattered toiletries. The room had an earthy, musky smell. It wasn't unbearable but, still, off-putting. It was all a lot. It felt as though my body had traveled across the ocean faster than my spirit, like I wasn't fully present yet. It was the same slip-slide feeling I used to get on drop-off day at overnight camp: smiling at people whose names I immediately forgot, choosing my bed and testing it for comfort in a fugue state, wondering about the girls I'd be sharing air with for the coming months, and knowing that everyone who felt comfortable and familiar was stopping for pizza without me before starting the two-hour drive home.

When I had set off on this strange adventure, it never occurred to me that, at thirty-four years old, I would suddenly be thrust back to the days of sharing a room with a stranger, navigating the uncomfortable sensation of having to sleep and dress with someone else's thoughts assessing me. My mind wandered back to the Rome roommate—the one who liked to dance topless—who had told me that I slept like a dead person. I stared at the blue backpack. It didn't *seem* like the accoutrement of someone overly aggressive.

Overwhelmed, I sat on the chenille bedspread, sinking deep into the old mattress and wondering what, exactly, I had set in motion. Out of habit, I put my feet flat on the floor, calming myself by breathing in and out. A visualization padded into my mind. Like I'd done a hundred times before, I imagined my feet growing roots that sunk and stretched as I dropped them deep into the loam of the Irish soil.

There was a tentative knock and the door swung open. I must have fallen asleep. The corner of my mouth felt crusty with drool. Perfect.

"You were sleeping. Sorry," said a quiet voice. Little light was coming through the window. I must have slept for hours. The woman in the doorway moved into the room, skirts swishing. "I'm Lucy." A patchwork satchel joined the pile on the bed. "Eleanor wants us in the dining room when you're ready." She dug in the backpack and pulled out a notebook. "See you out there," she said, closing the door behind her as she left.

Sitting up, I scrubbed my hands over my face and through my hair. The room was bigger than I'd first thought, with a window near the foot of Lucy's bed. Kneeling on the floor, I opened my suitcase and dug around for a clean sweatshirt. Was there time to unpack? I decided against it. My T-shirt smelled sweaty as I pulled it over my head. The sweatshirt smelled like nothing, and I relaxed a little. Shoes were left by the front door so, in my socks, I padded into the hallway. Where the hall intersected the foyer there was a low table with a tall glass lantern. Inside, a pillar candle flickered. I paused, trying to get my bearings. Straight or right?

"We're in here!" Eleanor called.

That would be "right," I thought, mapping the house in my mind.

The dining room table was round and dark like the new moon. Eleanor and Lucy were already seated in high-backed chairs.

"Welcome," Eleanor said as I joined them. She reached for the teapot, which sat on a tray along with honey, milk, and shortbread cookies. My stomach gave an excited kick. Lucy sipped from her mug as Eleanor poured tea into mine. It was thick and black. I added half a spoonful of honey and a splash of milk, forcing myself to pause for a moment before reaching for a biscuit.

Eleanor passed us each a piece of paper, a syllabus for our two months of study. We would be learning about herbs by body system, she explained, and studying biology and chemistry to gain an understanding of how the body worked and how herbs support it. Field trips to stone circles and sacred sites dotted the syllabus, as well as classes in astrology and biodynamic gardening. Clinic days were noted, during which we would observe Eleanor consulting with clients. Interestingly, moon phases were marked, as was the autumn equinox and the ancient Celtic holiday of Samhain, which falls near our modern Halloween. The course ended shortly thereafter. Looking at the syllabus, I realized I'd stepped into an alternate worldview, one that was as seamless and whole as the one I'd grown up with but based on a different set of foundational principles. Like the Gaia Theory I'd studied at New York University, this worldview seemed to posit that everything was connected: the herbs to the sacred sites, the sacred sites to the Celtic holidays, the Celtic holidays to the moon, and the moon to the herbs.

Lucy was nodding along. It didn't seem like this was foreign to her. But for me? It was a fresh beginning.

After dinner, we were back in the dining room. Eleanor had set up two chairs. In front of each, on the floor, was a towel with a large plastic bin set on it. The straight-backed chairs were plumped with pillows and throw blankets; the room was candlelit and soft. The scent of . . . geranium, *maybe?*, wafted through the air.

Eleanor was sitting on her knees, somehow looking like both a supplicant and a queen, her long hair sweeping the floor. In front of her, the tea tray had been transformed: it now held a small brazier and what looked like a bowl of oil-drenched salt. Gentle music, the kind Kate had used for yoga class, vibrated from invisible speakers.

Lucy and I had come into the room together. "Sit," Eleanor suggested as we entered, indicating the chairs. Lucy and I looked at each other. She was obviously baffled too.

As we moved toward the chairs, I could see there was water in the bins, steaming slightly. The steam was wafting the spicy, floral scent that permeated the space. I rearranged the pillows behind me while Eleanor moved to kneel by Lucy. Gently, almost reverently, Eleanor removed Lucy's socks and slid the bin up to the chair, before guiding Lucy's feet inside, first one, then the other.

"Relax," she murmured, gracefully shifting over to remove my socks. As she slid the basin close, the cinnamon scent of geranium washed over me. My discomfort warred with the warm water as she gently lowered my feet into the basin.

Through slitted eyes, I watched Eleanor light the charcoal in the brazier, dropping what looked like three golden pebbles onto the burning coal. Slowly, the room filled with the smell of frankincense, somehow both earthly and soaring. Then, one at a time, Eleanor knelt before us again, scooping oiled salt out of the bowl to scrub our feet. The candles flickered. She added more frankincense to the brazier, thickening the air.

I leaned back in the chair. The room was mostly dark, and the tending so unexpected. Time was difficult to keep in focus.

In minutes or hours, my feet were gently lifted and the basin slid away. The towel underneath was wrapped around my toes. And then Eleanor pulled her hair over her shoulder, a shimmering curtain in the candlelight, which she used to dab the remaining droplets from the tops of my feet. My mind was shorn. Tears puddled my eyes.

Standing up, Eleanor pulled a small vial from her pocket, tipping it onto her fingertip, which she laid on my brow between my eyes.

"Cleansed and anointed, you are welcome," she murmured.

Once she had done the same for Lucy, she bowed before us, hands in prayer position.

"Shhhhhh," she murmured. "It's time for sleep."

Bewildered and oddly gratified, we shuffled off to bed.

46

September 21, 2003

Re: The Irish Times

Yesterday, after running myself ragged trying to collect and tincture elderberry before the first frost, Eleanor (my teacher) introduced me to an Irish saying: *Come down off your cross, we need the wood.* So today I'm trying to move more slowly. . . .

Days are flying in a blur of garden work, lessons, tincturing, and road trips. I spend time each day hanging out with the cows in the back pasture. There is a bull that is fairly confrontational, but the rest of the herd seems happy to have me around.

We are learning to harvest by the moon. Plants are very sensitive to the moon's phases and sap runs differently at various times of the month. It takes a heightened awareness to always be conscious of what's happening in the night sky.

My only complaints are that it's difficult to find dark chocolate and I have to walk an hour and a half into town to use the internet.

Thank you for all your emails, I feel greatly loved sitting here at the computer.

So much love,

Maia

September 21, 2003

Re: P.S.

Dear Joanna, Francis, and Martha—

A smidge more for you, my magical friends:

Earlier this week we visited a place called the Piper's Stones. It's a prehistoric stone circle in the hills near Wicklow. We climbed a fence and braved a herd of sheep to get there. The stones speak in many different voices—old and crumbly, light and laughing. In the center of the circle is a hawthorn tree that is so old that she lays on her side.... But she still blooms. It was a magical day ... my mind was half in this world and half in the other realms.

I love the work I'm learning here. It is spiritual yet completely practical. Every day I must listen and connect with the wind and the trees and the flowers ... and put that concentration to specific purpose. At the end of the day, I have created medicines that will be used to help both people and animals. No matter how far my spirit travels in this process, I still feel more and more grounded and of the earth. The work suits me well.

The woman I'm studying with, Eleanor, is wonderful. She feels to me like a priestess ... and not of the airy-fairy pie-in-the-sky sort. It is as if she has reinvented the role of the priestesses of old: part of the community, yet separate; working alone and with others to bring the spirits of earth into daily life. (I know you will relate to this because it's what each of you does, too.) She works for many local causes as well as teaching, seeing clients, and tending the plants. And she tends to us, her students, as though we are the household princesses. Which is not to say we don't work, and work hard ... but then we sit down to lovely

193

meals by candlelight, luxuriate in the bath, and spray rose water on our pillows before bed. I am beginning to believe in everyday magic . . . and something more.

I miss you all, my sisters and fellow journeyers. I hope that I soak these lessons into my taproots so that I can share them with you when I return.

xo-

m.

47

Hindu legend tells the tale of a debate amongst the gods: Brahma, creator of the world, said that the lotus was the most beautiful flower of all, but Vishnu, protector of the world, claimed that accolade went to the rose.

Lucy and I collapsed onto the velvety green turf at the garden's center. I stretched my back gently, twisting one way and then the other. Harvesting was always more physically demanding than I expected, and I was looking forward to heading inside, putting my feet up, and having a cup of tea. (I was pretty much always looking forward to a cup of tea.)

"Before we go in, let's show a little gratitude and offer a blessing to the garden," Eleanor suggested.

I stared at her for a beat, baffled. The thirteen-year-old in me—the one who had a bat mitzvah only to keep her horseback riding privileges—was immediately on guard. *Really? I'm going to be forced to pray?* she growled. For years I'd purposely kept my language neutral. Words like *prayer* and *bless-ing* and *god* reminded me of religion. They reminded me of things I'd been coerced to do, things that made me feel like a hypocrite.

So I stuttered "Uhhhmmm . . . but, Eleanor, I'm not religious." Since I sounded like a sullen tween anyway, I added my best atheist glare.

Eleanor sighed, her expression surprisingly similar to my mom's "give me strength" look. Then she raised her eyes, studying the scuttling clouds and the circling crows. I suspect she was counting to ten—slowly. Maybe even backward. She pursed her lips and took a breath before speaking.

"Everyone," she enunciated, "has the right to bless."

Everyone has the right to bless.

Later that night, I noted her phrasing in my journal. Not "everyone can bless," or "everyone should bless." *Everyone has the right to bless.* This phrasing was somehow personal and inalienable. A blessing could be *mine.* It didn't have to be just repeated phrases from a prayer book. It wasn't owned by organized religion. Something clicked into place in my mind. Blessing aligned with the words I'd been murmuring for years—the love I'd showered on the Hudson River or Hazelton the Witch Hazel. I'd *been* blessing, I'd just avoided the term.

Back in the garden, Lucy had wandered toward the pond and was kneel-ing, her body relaxed and her eyes fixed on something low to the ground. Eleanor, however, remained a few feet from me, watching with the predatory patience of a hunting bird. I took a deep inhale, letting the scent of the apoth-ecary rose settle my mind. The flowers were loosely whorled and smelled like vetiver, warmed and sweetened by the sun. It was an old bush, taller than me and as wide as both of my arms outstretched. Snuggled up to the rose was a gunnera, a plant with leaves that were each bigger than a yoga ball. The two together formed a private nook in the garden. Most afternoons since I'd arrived, I'd sit in the alcove made by these two plants and write in my jour-nal while listening to the crows chortling and the cows lowing in the pasture behind the house.

The week before, Lucy and I had harvested about half the roses, laying the flowers upside down to dry in flat baskets that we arranged on shelves built into the small closet that housed the hot water heater. The warm, dry air and the dark of the closet quickly dehydrated the petals without bleaching their color. That evening, we'd chatted while pulling the dried pink flowers apart. There was something talc-like to the petals; they were papery but still silky on my fingertips. The scent seemed concentrated, as if the drying process—the removal of water—had condensed the molecules that made up the rose's scent, stacking them one atop the other and creating a richness that hadn't been there before. We dropped the petals into a tall mason jar, which we then stored in the dark recesses of the odd little room off the kitchen porch, which I affectionately called the herb closet. Those rose petals would be incorporated into the face cream Eleanor whisked by hand or added to teas for those with heart conditions—both physical and emotional. Some would end up in bath salts or incense or even, occasionally, an eyewash. A very special few would be placed, with loving care, into a sachet meant to go under the pillow of a mourner to ease dreams of love lost.

The irony of my adoration for this enormous old rosebush was not lost on me: I was a vehement and vocal hater of long-stemmed roses. They were boring, evidence of the failed imagination of their giver. But *Rosa gallica officinalis,* the apothecary rose, was nothing like the overbred, thorn-free, long-stemmed roses bandied about by florists and prom dates. This grande dame was lush and wild, with dark pink petals surrounding a sunshine-yellow center. Unlike her smooth-skinned sisters, the apothecary rose had glorious thorns and was happy to prick your finger if you mishandled her. Plus, she was ancient. This plant was thought to be the original Persian rose, and it was easy to imagine that rose water distilled from the apothecary rose had graced Cleopatra's vanity, that her scent had lingered on Eleanor of Aquitaine's wrist.

I was clearly falling for this plant. *What would it be like to offer her a blessing? To own the act of blessing in a way I'd never dared before?* I glanced at Lucy, but she was deep in her own meditations. Tentatively, I held up my hands, palms to the rosebush. I imagined sending everything I felt—all my love and awe and gratitude—down through my arms and out through my hands. I imagined whispering to the universe: *this rose is sacred to me.*

My hands began to heat up, to tingle a bit. The longer I stood sending my love to the plant, the stronger the sensation became. All that extra energy, the burning fizz I bound with words on the page, found a new channel. Like two magnets, the rose and I were being drawn together, energy circling and filling the space between us. It was a sensation of communion that reminded me of a state I would sometimes achieve while horseback riding: my breath and the horse's would sync up, the horse's movements seamlessly shifting my muscles and my muscles seamlessly triggering its movements. It was a sensation I thought I'd lost forever; something I'd believed I could only achieve with the horse I'd ridden as a teenager, a tall chestnut my parents had donated to Valley Forge Military Academy when I went away to college. Finding that feeling again was soul food. It was transcendence. It was love flowing in an electric loop.

It was, apparently, a blessing.

48

Anubis, the jackal-headed Egyptian god of death, carries a key that unlocks the underworld where he escorts the dead. Yet keys are also symbols of new beginnings: the key to a house, the key to your heart. Perhaps the secret to a key is that it knows that beginnings and endings are much the same.

Later in the week, while I was still marveling at my first real experience of blessing, we had a field trip. Piling into Eleanor's tiny black two-door, we headed north, winding through the cow pastures and hayfields. Though she'd grown up in the States, Eleanor drove like a native, racing along roads that hardly qualified as two lanes. We slowed slightly through the roundabout at Castlepollard, mustard and brick red buildings flashing by, before continuing onto Oldcastle. There, we pulled into a café built into the remains of an old mill. I thought we were just stopping for tea and to use the loo, but our rest stop turned out to be far more magical than that.

Eleanor, in head-to-toe cream—which hardly seemed an appropriate color for hiking, although that was what we'd been told we'd be doing—leaned against the counter, calling the barista by name. The proprietress sauntered over.

"Going up for a visit, are ye?"

"Thought I'd take the girls," Eleanor said, indicating the two of us. Lucy smiled and I murmured hello. "But maybe some tea first. And scones if you have them."

A few minutes later, the woman bustled over to the table we'd claimed, setting down a pot of tea, three cups, and a plate of round scones. Then she reached into the pocket of her apron and produced a key.

We parked in a lot near a placard that announced *Slieve na Calliagh*—meaning *the hill of the crone* (or *witch*, depending on the translation). Eleanor took the lead, her walking stick thumping at regular intervals. Lucy and I followed behind her.

When we got to the head of the trail, the hilltop flattened. In front of us was a barrow on the mountain's top. Eleanor walked surely over the grass and stone to the iron gate that was fitted into the mouth of the mound's passage-way. Fishing in her pocket, she pulled out the key she'd been given at the café. It slid into the keyhole and, with a moan, the gate swung open.

When I was studying in Rome during college, our archaeology profes-sor would often produce magical keys just like this one. We'd come to a gate tucked between buildings or a grate in a utility closet at some well-known tourist site, and he'd feel around in the pockets of his safari vest and pull out a sliver of metal. The gate would open, unlocking worlds most people would never see. Following the professor, the nine of us—a small summer class—would carefully navigate the empty archaeological sites buried beneath the bustle of the city. The stillness we found there was so complete it was hard to believe we were still in Rome. There were no children's voices echoing, no zealously applied cologne masking the scent of marble. It was on these tramps around Rome, visiting both sacred and secret sites, that I began to consider the possibility of becoming an architect, of creating spaces someone might sneak reverently into hundreds of years later.

Eleanor held open the gate. It would just be me going in—she wanted us each to feel the place for ourselves, undistracted by conversation or someone else's energy. The temperature dropped as I stepped over the threshold. Something deep in my core relaxed. There's a feeling I get from ancient stone; it's like being hugged by infinity. Maybe that's what Llorraine had meant when she called me an old soul—someone for whom the forgotten spaces feel like home.

After unlocking the gate, Eleanor had reached inside and flicked a switch. Safety lights guided me into the tomb with its Neolithic carvings of spirals and sun glyphs. At the spring equinox, the sun comes down the passage to light the interior, but at this moment it was dark.

I knew from my archaeological studies that I shouldn't touch the carvings, but I couldn't help myself. Pulling my sleeve over my hand to protect the rock from the oils on my skin, I gently traced the shapes carved thousands of years ago, thinking of the countless people who had stood where I did now, their fingers following the same curve of the lines. The shapes were right out of our symbolic dream worlds: a sun not just a star but a representation of our ability to see and find warmth, a horse not just an animal but a metaphor for personal power. This was my interior world, a world of symbol and meaning, miraculously given form. It was like I'd been turned inside out, the dream world now external, a cradle for my body.

Eventually, I heard Lucy's skirts swishing along the passage. Pressing my palms into prayer position, I bowed to each of the four directions, murmuring my thanks to those who had passed and those yet to come, who all seemed present at this crossroads of infinity.

49

In ancient times healers interpreted the curative properties of plants by examining their structure and shape, from the color of the leaves to the habits of their growth. This is called the Doctrine of Signatures. *It is the way that the plants communicate with us bumbling humans, who don't speak the language of wind and rain.*

Watching Eleanor work with clients was its own kind of magic. Her intake form was much like a doctor's, but what she got from the questions and their answers was completely different, like she was reading, not the words, but the space between them.

That day, a client sat at the dining room table, drinking tea from a cup that looked small in his hands. He was in his mid-twenties and his military bearing lent a formality to his jeans and T-shirt. Eleanor was questioning him closely about his deployments, getting very precise in her queries about different localities. I could tell she was tracking something, but I had no idea what.

There was a stack of pages on the table. His medical records. She thumbed through them, reaching to pull her readers down from where they rested on the top of her head. Lucy and I sat quietly as she cross-referenced lab tests from various dates.

Pulling two sheets out of the stack, Eleanor set them side by side. She ran a finger down one column, then glanced at the other sheet, aligning her findings.

Looking up, she took her readers off and put them on the stack, a slash of green across the white of the papers.

"Can you get a few more tests?" she asked, already writing a list.

"I think so. My doc's pretty open."

She handed him the sheet. Everything was written in abbreviations. It didn't mean anything to me.

"I have a suspicion. I want confirmation," Eleanor said.

Eleanor suspected the army ranger had picked up a fungus on one deployment, which had replicated exponentially when he was transferred to a hotter and more humid base. The tests came in a few weeks later, confirming her thoughts.

———————

As I walked the fields afterward, it occurred to me that Eleanor was using her intuition. She wasn't just letting random intutive information float in along with all the other sensory input, but instead she was turning intuition to a purpose, using it to find truths that had eluded the army ranger's medical doctors for months.

Mud squished under my boots. It had been drizzling for days. I tucked a damp curl behind my ear. Watching Eleanor, I sensed she used her intuition like a hound, letting it sniff around and then following it once it had caught the scent.

The sun was lowering, but I still had at least an hour of light. Eleanor had asked me to collect hawthorn berries before dinner. I glanced at the sun's position near the horizon. I had enough time for an experiment.

Standing in the middle of the field, I let my breathing even out and my spine straighten so that I was a conduit between earth and sky. My imaginary roots sunk into the earth, grounding down. And then I pictured chickweed, *Stellaria media,* with her tiny star flowers and tumbling oblong leaves. If you live in North America, you're familiar with this plant. It spills forth from abandoned planters and cracks in the sidewalk. In Ireland, it had eluded me.

Though I'd been sent to gather chickweed multiple times, I'd continually failed to find it. But I wondered what would happen if I let loose the hounds of *my* intuition. I stood still with my eyes closed and breathed, picturing the sweet little flowers. *Where are they?* I asked in my mind. Slowly, I turned my body until I felt a tug. Opening my eyes, I began walking, adjusting my path to follow my internal compass. The cows had cropped down and trampled the grass; the ground was soggy from the incessant rain. I was in the wrong boots for trekking across the field; my toes were already damp. But a thin silk had unspooled, and it tugged me forward. I was on the same web as chickweed; we were linked now.

If I had just been using my eyes, I never would have noticed it. The chickweed, always small, was tiny—miniscule even—the flowers hardly bigger than the head of a pin. Still, I crouched down in the damp, ruffling its little leaves, a grin splitting my face.

"YES!" I crowed. "YES, YES, YES!"

Three cows stopped grazing to swing their heads my way, their liquid eyes soft and accepting before they returned to their munching.

———————

In Ireland, hawthorns are grown in hedgerows that define the edges of fields and attempt to keep the cows from neighboring pastures. As I swung my basket, I walked along the hedge so I could gather berries on the way back to the house.

Occasionally you'll see a lone hawthorn tree, twisting and turning itself into fantastical shapes. This is a Faerie Tree—a portal to the other world. The Irish are superstitious about these trees. It's terrible luck to cut one down. Every town has a tale of someone who tried to get away with clearing a hawthorn to make way for a garage or chicken coop. In these tales, the lucky ones end up in the hospital; the not so lucky, in the graveyard.

Finding a patch of berries the birds hadn't decimated, I put my basket on the ground so I could weave my fingers through the hawthorn's long, bony spikes. With my hands suspended amid the branches, I suddenly remembered I was supposed to ask, not just take willy-nilly. Extracting my hands, I stepped back. And then back again. I felt like I had to reapproach. Start over. The trees seemed to approve, to be waiting.

"Hi, friends," I murmured. And then, using my inner voice, I asked if they would share the harvest. I thought about Eleanor's clients, the ones I'd met who would receive the hawthorn medicine to heal their heartaches. The berries began to look a little brighter, ripe and soft-skinned, as though the low-hanging clouds had lifted and the sun was picking them out one by one. I stepped up again and began to fill the basket. The thorns parted to let my fingers pass.

———————

Marjoram and thyme mingled with garlic in the warm air of the kitchen. Lucy was in charge of dinner. I swung the basket onto the counter and stripped off my coat. It was heavy and damp as I hung it on a hook behind the door. Eleanor was at the dining room table, garbling something on long stalks, maybe motherwort. She deftly removed the leaves, piling them into a big bowl.

"You're soaked," she called. "Go change."

I grabbed one of the towels we kept on the coatrack, blotting my hair as I crossed through the dining room and headed toward the bedrooms.

"There are a couple dead birds under the power lines," I told Eleanor as I passed. I thought maybe she'd call the electric company, that perhaps something was wrong with the lines.

"Umm," Eleanor said. I kept walking. When I was almost to the hall, she continued, throwing her voice to be sure that I heard, "Sounds like it's time you learned to deal with death."

I froze, the towel mid-scrunch in my curly hair.

"What?"

Eleanor twisted in the chair so she could meet my eye. "It's time you learned to deal with death. You found the birds; they're yours to deal with."

203

I was startled and wanted to protest, but in my mind, I heard the voice from my dream, the one that had sent me to Ireland: *go and study the birds.*

At the back of the garden, behind the gunnera and the apothecary rose, I built a cairn with stones I carried from the pasture. I laid each bird-body in a small rock-room, and then covered it with a larger stone, hiding the body from view. I picture them there sometimes, a cloister of wings and feathers. Over the course of my stay at Eleanor's, the cairn got taller and taller, as if the birds knew I would honor them and so came close to die.

I wish I could tell you I was a gracious priestess, gently cradling the small, winged forms and carrying them to their final resting place. Instead, I cursed and squealed as they fell off the shovel; my gorge rose when I tried to pick them up and they suddenly disintegrated. But with each bird, something settled in me. I began, slowly, so slowly, to step into the fullness of life's cycle, not just as a metaphor, but as a part of my reality: beginnings and endings, life and death, over, and over, and over again. Each phase is unique and necessary if the wheel is to keep turning.

50

On Samhain night, when the veils are thin, an offering plate can be left out for any spirits who might be abroad. Traditionally, the plate was filled from your own table: a sharing of your own repast. In this way, you honor those of your blood lineage as well as those who have passed from your life.

The knife flashed and the apple fell in two halves, cut not stem-to-stern but instead horizontally. In the apple's core were seeds in the shape of a star. Eleanor used the knife to dig them out.

"These seeds represent your intentions for the coming year," Eleanor said as she handed a small pile to each of us. "Think on what you'll nurture; what you want to grow."

It was November 1, the first day on the Celtic calendar. I'd been harboring an intention for the new year, tending its tiny flame, but I wasn't ready to speak it aloud. Instead, I tucked my seeds into the pocket of my jeans. Eleanor noticed and nodded.

"That actually smells good," I said as the subtle scent of apple wafted through my hangover fog. Eleanor cut the apple into chunks. I nabbed one from the cutting board, chewing slowly, letting the sweet and tart curl over my tongue. It reminded me of the apples we ate with honey at Rosh Hashanah. Growing up, I'd been told we dipped apples in honey for a sweet year. The symbolism of the seed—of growing something—deepened the metaphor. I reached for another slice just as Lucy did; our hands bumped. She laughed, moving snake-fast to snatch the piece she wanted.

Last night had been Halloween in the modern world, "Samhain" in the Celtic one. The week leading up to the holiday was a mad rush of harvesting and medicine making. Eleanor told us that on Samhain night the fairies piss on the garden, so you must do the final gathering before then. Whether you believe in fairies or not, it's a lovely tradition to leave some of the berries and seeds on your plants for small critters who also need winter sustenance.

The promise of the past night's party had carried us through the week of work that preceded it. That, and discussing what we would wear.

Samhain marked the end of the harvest and the descent into the shadow time of year. It stood as a gateway into the darkness. The idea entranced me, and I decided, for my costume, to let my own shadow-self rise to the surface. I would dress as Autumn Ending. I'd been gathering raven feathers to braid into my hair and saving the remains of the charcoal discs we used for incense so I could mix a black paint to band across my eyes.

"Anyone else want water?" I moved into the kitchen, pulling glasses from the cupboard. I'd only slept a few hours and my eyes were gritty and dry—perhaps from the charcoal but likely from the alcohol. Once I had painted my face and Lucy had braided the feathers into my hair, I became something other, a fae creature, a goddess for a night. A thick leather belt held my layered skirts, all in shades of black and brown, like the murky waters of the Irish peat bogs. As we slid into the twilight of the year, the effect was neither pretty nor silly; it was potent.

Cars had pulled into the driveway, depositing other timeless creatures, each sketched with the pen of deep imagination. Incense was thick in the air—frankincense, vervain, and petals from the apothecary rose. The storytelling started, and the bodhran kept a steady beat. Once I'd had a glass of wine or two, it felt like we were between the worlds and not quite physical beings anymore. The veil was thin, and we mere spirits passing through.

It was well after one in the morning when the bodhran player slid his drum into its canvas case, and later still by the time everyone said their farewells and got sorted into cars. I started to tidy as people were leaving, gathering discarded cups from the mantel and the coffee table, but Eleanor said to leave it. Lucy was asleep by the time I cleaned my face. Undoing the braids, I sensed my modern-self overwriting my mythic one; she faded into the background as the smoke left my eyes and the feathers fell out of my hair.

I stared at my bare face. Which was real and which was costume?

———————

That night I dreamed I was the earth. Lying on my side, my hip became a hillside, my shoulder a mountain range. I wasn't separate; I was one.

———————

On the morning of November 1, I awoke at 6:30, my usual time. No one else was up as I padded barefoot down the hall. Stopping before Eleanor's altar in the foyer, I knelt. The setup was simple. It held only a lantern and candle, which Eleanor changed before it could gutter, one candle lighting the next. Sometimes there was a bowl of incense, sometimes a vase of flowers. Airmid, the ancient Irish goddess of herbs and healing, was the household deity. While I didn't feel a personal relationship with her, it was Airmid's sanctuary in which I was dwelling. I stared at the flame, thinking through all I was grateful for: the learning I'd received in the ways of plants and the healing of humans, the magic of the herb closet with its hanging bundles and steeping potions, the quiet time to remember myself, the connection I felt with this ancient land. *Thank you,* I whispered, before getting to my feet.

The altar was about the only surface that wasn't sporting a cup sticky with last night's cordials or dandelion wine. *First the magic, then the mopping,* I thought, beginning to gather them up. And that too is how it should be. We don't live just in one world; we live in both: the mythic and the material.

As that thought flickered across my mind, it dawned on me: After a lifetime of looking, I'd finally stepped into my own story. I'd found the magic I'd been looking for.

My heart felt huge, leaving me almost breathless as I glanced back at the flickering candle on the altar. Blotting my eyes, I sent another wave of gratitude to the household goddess, then took a deep breath to reground myself and got back to work.

Once I had picked up the discarded cups, I eased open the kitchen door. I'd forgotten to grab socks when I left the bedroom, so stuffed my pajama bottoms into my boots to keep my ankles warm.

The fog, omnipresent at this time of day, wouldn't burn off for a few hours. The small glasshouse next to the pond had half disappeared and there was only mist beyond the pasture gate. On mornings like this, when the world slipped in and out of focus, it was easy to believe in fairies and leprechauns.

Pulling the sleeves of my jacket down over my fingers, I crossed the drive, gravel rolling underfoot. It sounded loud and I imagined shushing my feet: *Shh! Eleanor and Lucy are sleeping!* I smiled. Maybe I was still a little drunk.

Trying to make my steps noiseless, I wound into the garden's center. Yesterday evening, before the revelers arrived, we had followed the same route. Our small procession—just me, Lucy, and Eleanor—had placed plates of food at the base of the elderberry tree. I crouched down next to my offering, silently calling to any ancestors who might be abroad on Samhain night. I listed my dead: all my grandparents, both my mother's brother and my father's, my grandma's sister Ceil, who had a hand in my raising, my childhood friend Cheryl, who was born with a broken heart. . . . In the twilight, with my hands on the earth, it seemed I could feel the wheel of time turning, the darkness of the year taking hold. According to Eleanor, the tradition of laying out food for the dead on Samhain, the final day of the Celtic year, had morphed into a tradition I was more familiar with: handing out candy on Halloween. Both were meant to appease spirits that might be wandering the darkness.

Like a kid wondering if Santa had visited, I wanted to see what remained on the plate I'd put out. Would the food be gone? Or was it like when Aunt Gloria put out wine for Elijah at Passover, a symbolic offering only? Thinking the plate might be empty was highly irrational. But I'd come to learn there was more to life than what my rationality had previously allowed for. And my life was more enjoyable for that realization. Anyway, there were plenty of critters who might have stopped by for a bite, if my brain insisted on a logical explanation.

As I moved through the garden, I collected empty plastic cups, the scent of red wine and Smithwick's making me a bit queasy. I had a small stack of them by the time I rounded the rosemary. There was the elderberry, already looking the crone with her berries picked and leaves shriveled. At her base were three plates, empty but for a smear of something red, maybe tomato sauce.

When I got back inside, carrying a tower of cups and the stacked plates I'd brought in from the garden, Eleanor and Lucy were up. The smell of coffee filled the kitchen. I gratefully took the mug Lucy offered, swapping her for the plates, which she put in the sink.

Eleanor was at the dining room table in a polar fleece robe. She held her coffee cup as though it might escape, clutching it with both hands.

When Lucy and I joined her, she picked up a knife from a cutting board she'd set in the center of the table. The apple was a dusky scarlet, not supermarket perfect. It was probably from a neighbor's tree. Eleanor sliced it in half, revealing the star. It was a new year.

Lucy had gone to get dressed. Eleanor was in the small kitchen, putting away the dishes Lucy had washed. I stood in the doorway, making up my mind. Scenes from the past few months flickered past: Learning how to make face cream with a whisk. ("Faster! Use your wrist!" Eleanor admonished.) Lucy howling after she spilled spaghetti water on her hand; Eleanor had grabbed her wrist and shoved it under the tap. Cold water, then lavender oil, cold water, then lavender oil, until her skin was pink instead of red. New moon meals, which were always dark colored—beet salads and purple kale with blackberry cobbler for dessert. There was a rhythm here that made sense to my soul, even if it did sometimes feel silly to my modern mind. The things I struggled with in other places—my overactive imagination, my highly sensitive intuition—were assets here. Or maybe, I should say, *here* I was learning how to make them into assets.

I fingered the apple seeds I'd put in my pocket. I'd been thinking about it for a while, what I wanted in the new year. I had even spoken with Eleanor a bit. An apple seed rolled smoothly between my thumb and forefinger. I remembered when Gail had told me I didn't need to see her anymore, then the knowing I felt that she still had more to teach me, the sense that she was a gatekeeper at the beginning of my journey. How do you know when one jour-

209

ney is over and the next begins? Or do they just roll into each other, journey, upon journey, upon journey as you build a life?

———————

"Eleanor?" I knew she could hear the question in my voice. She turned off the faucet. I took a step into the room. There was a shimmer in the air. It was the first silk, a glistening silvery thing, waving on an invisible wind, searching for a place to anchor.

I grounded down into my feet, dropping my roots right through the tiles of the kitchen floor. Taking a deep breath, I exhaled my intention for the year. "I want to stay."

Eleanor seemed frozen for a moment, or maybe that was just me, holding my breath. We'd discussed it already, the possibility of me continuing on. We were both thinking . . . deciding. Eleanor's hands were on the sink, her face hidden by a waterfall of glossy black hair. I stood still, waiting, letting her choose.

When she turned, she looked at the edges of me, making some unfathomable calculation. For a moment, she was the gatekeeper, the goddess of interstitial spaces, reading the patterns. Then her face softened, and she nodded once, like she was bowing her head. A blessing, a benediction . . .

The formal moment passed, and she stepped forward to give me a hug.

Out of the corner of my eye, I saw the anchor line shimmer.

A new weaving had begun.

Coda

Time upon time upon time, there was . . .

and is . . .

and will be . . .

a witch.

The witch lives in the depths of the dark forest. . . .

The witch lives in a cottage by the sea. . . .

The witch lives deep within our psyches, where she quietly goes
about the work of the cycles and the seasons, teaching us,
over and over again, the joy of letting magic in.

Acknowledgments

DURING MY FINAL WEEKS IN IRELAND, MY TEACHER AND I TRAVELED to many of my favorite sites so I could say my farewells. At one of them, a double stone circle we'd dubbed The Sun and Moon, I found a small, drilled rock, perfect for threading on a cord. I was thrilled: I thought the island was offering me a going-away gift. But when I put it on a thong around my neck, something felt off; I knew it wasn't for me. I sat with the small stone for a few days before realizing it was meant for Gail. When I returned to the States, I made the long drive to her new home in Vermont. Gail was delighted. "Stones are always getting us humans to carry them where they want to go," she told me.

That was the last time I saw her. It was 2005. Eleven years later, she died of a sudden brain aneurysm at fifty-one. Luckily, Gail left her teachings behind in two beautiful books, *Wood Becomes Water* and *Earth Acupuncture*. I turn to these when I need a bit of her wisdom.

Llorraine, fortunately, is still sharing her wisdom. In a 2022 email she told me she'd been thinking about how to describe her work in the world. She wrote, "I am not a psychic as much as I am the voice of Psyche during the session. So, I have decided to refer to myself as a *Medial Woman*, a woman who walks through the worlds bringing messages. . . . " I am forever grateful for the messages she carried to me.

While Gail and Llorraine's counsel marked the beginning of my journey, many others have contributed along the way. I would not be who I am without the love and support of the women known in this book as Annette and Quinn. How rare it is to have friends who take your spiritual tribulations as seriously as the usual ups and downs of daily life. While I am no longer in touch with either, I hope this book finds its way into their hands and they feel the immensity of my love. Eleanor and I were two strong-minded women locked in the deep relationship that apprenticeship requires; I think it's safe to say it was equal parts rewarding and frustrating for both of us. It got rocky toward the end, so I am always immensely grateful when she pops into my messages to tell me she's proud of who I've become.

After many years of working as a clinical herbalist and sharing plant lore with my own students, I embarked on a new journey—the author's journey. Writing books has both its own magic and its own special guides:

My agent Laura Lee Mattingly didn't know what this book would become but still trusted that I would figure it out. Hearing her tell me that the finished manuscript was both writerly and an easy read is a compliment I will carry close to my heart for a long time to come.

My editor Shannon Connors Fabricant has nurtured both my writing and my creativity in ways that make me feel seen and supported. Which is pretty much the vibe I get from the entire Running Press crew—Melanie, Ashley, Susan, Ada, Amy, Elizabeth, Kara, and Betsy. It feels amazing to be a part of this incredible team. Thank you all for helping me refine and express my vision, to know when to compromise and when to push ahead. You are my superstars!

Carrie and Paige aka The East Asheville Writing Triangle: You two are my Annette and Quinn, author-style. Thank you for celebrating every little moment of this manuscript, for going over and over (and over!) the writing, for saying things seventeen different ways until I understood, for countless cups of Earl Grey, for pointing out the themes I couldn't see and the spelling errors I would have missed. I, quite literally, couldn't have done it without you.

Steph, I learned to write a memoir by following the bread crumbs you laid down in your editorial comments. So many thanks for helping me under- stand how to create a hierarchy and structure for the manuscript. You saw the web before I did—I will be forever grateful you called in spider medicine! I forget, sometimes, that we live a country away from each other; you always feel close. XO.

Sarah: *The white tip of his tail disappeared into the rhododendron thicket.* The scene got cut, but your response to it gave me my initial understanding of what will resonate for the reader; it became my North Star. Charlotte, Kate, and Barbara: so many thanks for final edits and cheering me across the finish line.

Finally, life continues while an author stares at her computer rearranging words and sentences. Shannon, you always keep it flowing behind the scenes. Thank you for all the fires you put out before I even catch a whiff of smoke. You give me the gift of being able to work without distraction. Thank you.

Special thanks to my family, who lived all this with me. It wasn't easy for any of us, and yet we all still choose each other again and again. Love you.

And Andrew, my love and partner in all things, who encourages me, every day, to ride the silken threads and see where they land, to choose new anchor points, and to never be scared to spin a fresh web.